One hund

LEGEND

TONY PARKES

THE AUTHORISED BIOGRAPHY

WITH SUZANNE GELDARD

HERO BOOKS

PUBLISHED BY HERO BOOKS
DUBLIN
IRELAND

www.herobooks.digital

Hero Books is an imprint of Umbrella Publishing
First Published 2023
Copyright © Suzanne Geldard
All rights reserved

A CIP record for this book is available from the British Library

ISBN 9781910827673

Cover design and formatting: jessica@viitaladesign.com
Photographs: The Parkes Family Collection, *The Lancashire Telegraph*

CONTENTS

FOREWORD

Sir Kenny Dalglish

TONY PARKES WAS paramount to me joining Blackburn Rovers. He was part of the package. Without Tony there would not have been promotion; there would be no Premier League title – not the way we did it anyway.

The important thing for me in wanting to work with him was Tony's knowledge and respect within Blackburn.

That was really important for me. It was important for everybody, that everybody knew exactly what they were doing.

He was vital for us. He had seen everything, and that's vital. It's important that somebody knows the football club, knows the people who come to support the football club – what their expectations are, what they live up to, and what they enjoy – and, even more importantly, what goes on in and around the pitch because the better you do on the pitch the better and the larger your support is going to be.

If you're going to win the Premier League, it's not about one person, it's *everybody*; players, staff, the whole lot… owners, directors. Everybody. Everybody makes a contribution. And Tony made a vital contribution.

What does Tony Parkes mean to me?

For what he did, not just for the football club but for me being part and parcel of the football club, I gained benefit from it as well, working alongside him, with his contribution to the club in every aspect you could think of – welcoming you in, being approachable, carrying on the work he did, the information he gave us, the respect the players who came in had for Tony as well. It all contributed.

We were a team. The team behind the team.

There were three of us, with Ray Harford as well, and there was absolutely no animosity or no league table amongst the staff that somebody was more important than the other, and that's why it worked so well. We just all got on really well and did our jobs as well as we could, and everybody enjoyed it.

Tony was hugely instrumental and played a huge part in the success that we had.

And on top of that, he was a great person to work with.

A great person all round.

There was nobody, but *nobody* who had anything but very kind words to say about Tony, and deservedly so.

PREFACE

Suzanne Geldard

I HAVE BEEN a sports journalist for over 20 years. None of it might have been possible had it not been for Tony Parkes.

I'd decided at a very early age that when I grew up I wanted to write about football.

When all my peers were off doing exciting things for their Duke of Edinburgh Award Scheme, taking in outdoor adventures or going to theme parks in our Year 10 activities week – including Tony's daughter, Natalie – I was with a handful of others putting the school newspaper together.

We had a tour of Ewood Park that Tony had helped to arrange, and while we were there he not only agreed to an interview himself but also set up a couple of others for me with a current and former player.

During the course of writing Tony's story I messaged Natalie and wrote, 'I can't remember if I've ever told you this but if it wasn't for your dad I don't know if I'd have ever trodden this career path. He was such a massive help to me with the school newspaper'.

I went on to explain the story, and also told her about the time he'd distributed some questionnaires among the playing staff for my home economics coursework. I'm no chef by any means, but that survey about nutrition in sport – what top flight footballers put into their bodies to fuel them – put me on the path to an A grade.

Natalie replied, 'I never knew that. He loved to help where he could. I miss that side of him'.

I'm sure being school pals and hockey teammates with Natalie had a big say in how accommodating Tony was with our school assignment; knowing who I was and the purpose the project served.

But still, his time, co-operation and patience meant everything. When we had finished our interviews he even said he'd like to read it once it was printed. Tony Parkes wanted to read my first published work!

Rovers were preparing for the 1994/95 Premier League season – they would go on to be crowned champions. They had bigger fish to fry, but the players took time to speak to me and Tony instigated it all.

Ending the message I wrote, 'I owe him'.

This is one of the reasons why I wanted to write this book. I also wished to write it for Natalie, to unearth stories and anecdotes that she might never have heard before; to leave a lasting legacy for Tony's two beautiful grand-daughters, Elsie-Mae and Matilda; and to help the family by raising money to contribute to Tony's ongoing care as he lives with this cruel disease.

Tony has helped many people over many years. Now it is our turn to give something back, by sharing some of the memories of his life and his career that he is sadly no longer able to.

MY DAD

Natalie Parkes-Thompson

TO THE FOOTBALL world he is Mr Blackburn Rovers. To me, he is quite simply dad.

He was the one who taught me how to ride a bike. He was the one who used to take me swimming to Darwen Leisure Centre on a Sunday morning and we'd have a raspberry Slushie and a packet of puff crisps from the vending machine straight after. They were ready salted and tasted of nothing, but... this is my abiding memory of my childhood. Sunday was the day I spent with dad, and that's what we did.

It was not what you might consider a conventional childhood.

I didn't know any different, of course. But having children of my own now I have made sure that we have done the things that I essentially missed out on, like weekend trips to the seaside and going camping. It was not that he and my mum, Eileen, didn't want to do these things, it's just that the opportunity wasn't there.

Growing up in a football bubble, our weekends and school holidays were quite different to those of my friends. As for summer holidays? They were condensed in to a two-week window before pre-season started… and dad had to go back to work.

Sunday was our day, for Dad and I, because that was his only time off.

I'm not sure he would have had it any other way. As much as he loved me and my mum, outside of family football was his life. And he was good at it. His longevity at Blackburn Rovers as a player, with 409 appearances to his name, and as a coach and six-time caretaker manager is testament to that.

He would not have worked with a succession of managers, including Kenny Dalglish, Roy Hodgson and Graeme Souness – and shared in the club's successes – had that not been the case.

But there were sacrifices along the way. There still are. That's why this book is so important to me and my family.

Dad was diagnosed with Alzheimer's in November, 2019.

I'm sure that football is a contributing factor to it; heading footballs, balls that were much heavier than they are now, especially when they were wet. And I'm certain that losing mum in October, 2009, less than a year after she was diagnosed with bone cancer, was an accelerator to this horrible disease.

Mum's passing hit us both really hard, and dad slowly but surely began to withdraw from the activities he had previously enjoyed.

Memories are locked away in his head now, unable to get out. Memories of his brilliant career. Twice winning promotion from the Third Division – once as champions. As a coach, helping

Rovers become founding members of the Premiership, and going on to win the title itself. Then adding the Worthington Cup to the trophy cabinet, having also contributed to the Full Members' Cup win much earlier on in his coaching career.

He can no longer tell his story, but it is a story that is more than worthy of being told, and as a collective we have done it for him as best we can.

I am eternally grateful to those who have shared their memories of dad's life and career in football to put the pieces of the jigsaw together to make a lasting legacy for his two granddaughters – my daughters Elsie-Mae and Matilda.

They adore dad, and he adores them, and it is wonderful to be able to tell his story to them.

CHAPTER 1

The Early Years

TONY PARKES WAS born on May 5, 1949 – the third of five children and middle son of Arthur and Hilda.

Like his siblings, June, Ron, Graham and Hilary, Tony was born at home, and the family was raised in the steel city of Sheffield.

School playing fields that backed on to their three-bedroomed house on The Manor estate were like a giant green magnet to Tony. At every given opportunity he would grab his football and play. Even if there was no-one to play with he would go out and practice dribbling and shooting. But more often than not he would be accompanied by one or both of his brothers and neighbours from their housing estate on Pipworth Road.

School did not really interest Tony. He went because he had to, and he left at the earliest opportunity, when he was 15 years old. He was never academic, but Tony's football education, and temperament, set him apart.

He excelled for the school teams, and town and county teams. He was released from Rotherham's youth team, but never gave up on his dream, and having earned a reputation as a prolific goalscorer, was signed by Buxton.

Tony completed his apprenticeship as a wall and floor tiler and earned £30 a week from his day job, and a further £7 a game.

He had met a young lady called Eileen Barry, from Stocksbridge, and they were planning a life together. Nevertheless, he took a pay cut when Blackburn Rovers came calling – a significant one having been offered a £25 a week deal – but it was a price worth paying for becoming a professional footballer.

Rovers paid Buxton £3,000. What a bargain!

They had bought Tony Parkes for life.

◄◄◄ • ►►►

Graham Parkes
(Tony's youngest brother)

WE WERE A close-knit family. All three of us brothers especially were close, which is just as well because we all shared a room at one time, with one double bed and one single bed.

Getting off to sleep used to be a nightmare.

I was the youngest, with two older brothers who insisted on playing 'last touch' before you went to sleep. You'd be laid there and then... the next minute someone would tap you on the foot so you had to leave it 10 minutes... and you'd have to sneak up on them to get them back. It went on for hours because whoever got the last touch won, and we were all competitive.

When my oldest sister, June, moved out, Ron moved into his own room and everyone moved round a little bit.

Our grandad, William Bunting, lived with us for quite a few years after our grandma, Florence, died. Being a miner, he had some good tales to tell. I think he probably still holds the record for being the longest serving miner. I can remember him getting a certificate for 60 years from the MCB.

He was quite a character.

None of us followed him down the pit. Tony took up tiling and did his apprenticeship at a company called Rigby's and then he worked for a guy called Philip Skelton, who we played football with.

All three of us brothers played football. Ron and Tony played together for years with different teams. There was a group of them, all local lads, who seemed to move from one team to another en masse.

I was a bit younger so I used to support for a while early doors every weekend – me and my youngest sister, Hilary – until I was old enough to start playing myself and then add to an already mountainous washing pile.

Tony and Ron used to play on Saturdays and Sundays, much to my mum's horror because they used to bring the kit home to be washed. And the pitches weren't as good as they are now so every week you could guarantee you'd be muddied from head to toe.

The kits would be in buckets, soaking in cold water overnight and then on Monday the whole day was taken up with washing. With five kids and a husband and all this football kit, you couldn't move in our house for washing at the beginning of the week. We must have had the longest washing line! It's a good job we had a big garden.

And then it wasn't until about Thursday that it had all dried and been ironed… and then starting all again at the weekend.

When we weren't playing football we were watching it, and Tony – like me – supported Sheffield Wednesday. Me and Tony were Sheffield Wednesday, and Ron was Sheffield United. Whenever we asked my dad who he supported he always said, 'York City' even though he only went to York to do his National Service. I think he just said that to sit on the fence so he didn't have to take sides.

With Ron and Tony being older than me, they used to take it in turns to take me with them to matches. I'd go to Bramall Lane one week, and then the week after I'd go to Hillsborough. And I ended up sticking with Sheffield Wednesday. We stood on the Leppings Lane End, which at the time was just a big terrace with a big roof over it, and an old fashioned scoreboard on the top.

Albert Quixall was Tony's favourite player. He was a classy midfield player who became a British record signing when he left Sheffield Wednesday for Manchester United for £45,000 in 1958.

Tony liked anybody with a bit of style.

As a player himself, Tony was a prolific centre-forward when he was younger.

He used to play in the Sheffield Sunday League and they had a representative side, and one day they played a side from the Manchester Sunday League. I went to that game. Sheffield won 6-0, and Tony scored all six goals.

He had a different role at Blackburn, but he was just happy being involved. I think he would have played in goal if he'd had to. I think it was his engine that encouraged them to turn him into a midfielder when he moved to Blackburn.

I used to race him. Our house backed onto a football pitch with big fields and woods, and he'd say to me, 'I'll race you to the changing rooms and back'. Oh crikey, when I got back I couldn't speak and Tony wasn't even out of breath. He was a natural runner, a natural athlete.

And he was an all-round sportsman.

He played cricket in the summer with Ron and myself and all the lads he played football with for a team called Woodland View, because it was something to do. 'There's no football, right... we'll play cricket!' And that's how it went.

Tony was a batsman, and he was good at it. But his first love was always football. From a very early age he started playing for Sheffield Boys and Yorkshire Boys.

We all had the same fantastic sports teacher at secondary school, a man called John Wilkinson, who later went on to run Sheffield School Sports. He had an influence on Tony especially. He would always push Tony. Mum and dad never pushed him, they were quite happy that if you liked doing something, great, but they would never push in one direction or the other.

Tony had huge respect for John Wilkinson, as did everyone else who met him. He was a lovely character.

I'd bump into him years later and he'd always ask how we were.

A Sheffield Boys game interrupted our holiday once. Mum and dad used to have a caravan on the east coast just outside

Skegness, and Tony had been picked to represent Sheffield at Hull, but we were away. Tony didn't miss the match though as we all drove from Skegness, and this was before the Humber Bridge was built so we had to catch the ferry to get across.

The problem was, we were downstairs and the portholes were under water and it was terrifying. And Tony was never a good traveller at the best of times. It used to take about two hours to get to Skegness in the car from where we lived, but with Tony it took three hours because we had to make about four stops.

It's amazing how much he travelled with work considering, especially when Blackburn got into Europe! It's the kind of thing you grow out of as you get older, but Tony never did.

After he joined Blackburn, I travelled all over the north watching him. I had a motorbike at the time so would go to places like Leicester, but also I spent a lot of time on the train, up to Manchester Piccadilly then across to Victoria to catch the train to Blackburn.

And I can remember him playing against my team, Sheffield Wednesday, at Hillsborough. Myself and Ron took mum and dad along as well, and Tony scored. They were going crazy, jumping up. People were telling them to sit down.

I didn't see him play as much after I started a family of my own. Life takes you in different directions and Tony was settled in Blackburn with Eileen, with Natalie arriving a few years later.

I can't remember how he proposed, but they must have worked the wedding around football because Tony was at Blackburn when they got married and I'm sure it was on a Saturday in the summer – during the closed season.

They were married at the registry office in Sheffield because Eileen was Catholic and Tony wasn't and I think it probably was the best option. Then they had the reception at my sister June's pub, The Big Tree. There was a big function room upstairs and they had weddings on all through the summer, so it was quite a good place to hold it. It was a lovely family occasion, a lovely day.

Tony had made a lovely life for himself at Blackburn, and the club became his life.

When Jack Walker came on the scene it changed everything. But Tony's love for the club never changed and the two had a really close bond, and a mutual respect, which was fantastic.

Ron Parkes
(Tony's oldest brother)

TONY WAS BORN for a career in football.

As a player growing up, I always thought he was so much better than everyone else.

He was an all-round player. Even though he scored lots of goals in amateur football, he could play anywhere. If we were short in defence he could drop in and he wouldn't be out of his depth at all.

We went to the same school. He played for school teams when he was four years younger than the others he was playing with. When he was in Senior One he was playing in the Senior Four football team.

By the time I got to be Senior Four level, Tony had already been playing in that team for three years!

He was an exception to the rule because he was so much better than most others.

We played on Sundays for a team called Arbourthorne Community Centre and won a couple of cups while we were there. And we played for a team on Saturdays called Sheffield Waterworks in quite a high level of football and won a couple of leagues with them too.

I was a central defender.

When Tony played with me, he was always a forward. A striker. He scored lots of goals. But when he signed for Blackburn Rovers they converted him into a midfield player.

He never played as a striker for Blackburn from what I remember, but he was comfortable with it. But I was amazed he never went in as a striker because they'd signed him based on how he'd played in that role.

When he played in the local teams with me he was signed by Buxton in the Cheshire League and played a season with them and scored 30 goals. He was setting records for goalscoring.

But all the family were really thrilled with his move to Blackburn, especially after the minor setback he had experienced after leaving school.

Tony wasn't academic. None of us were really. We were in Secondary Modern Schools – none of the family passed the 11-plus to get to grammar school or anything like that. We were just very ordinary.

So when Tony got signed from school for Rotherham, it was a dream come true.

They took him on as a 15-year-old and he played in the

Northern Intermediate League side, but when he got too old for that they released him. They said he wasn't big enough, and he went back to junior football for a short time. He was really disappointed, but he never stopped playing. He never said he wasn't going to bother. He found other teams to play for instead and did his apprenticeship to become a tiler, and went semi-professional with Buxton in the Cheshire League.

It didn't faze him, juggling the two. We had been brought up not knowing anything other than hard work with the example set by our parents.

Our dad, Arthur, worked seven days a week, right up to retiring. He worked all week and every weekend. He operated heavy machinery as a steel worker, making tools. We only saw him in the evenings. He was an early starter and a late finisher.

So it's a sort of family trait, not being afraid of hard work. And he had to work hard because there were five of us – three boys and two girls, with 20 years between the eldest, June and the youngest, Hilary. Our mother, Hilda had other jobs too as well as looking after us. She used to work in a pub in the evenings.

Myself and Tony were the closest in age of all our siblings with just three years between us, and we did everything together.

Before he got signed by Blackburn we played for the same teams in amateur football, and he must have been the main reason why we kept winning things.

At home we used to get into a bit of trouble now and again, egging each other on instead of going to sleep.

Sometimes, when me and my wife are talking now and a place name comes up she'll say to me, 'Do you remember when we went there and Tony did this or Tony did that... Tony was wearing a silly hat or signing that song'.

I remember one pub where we all got together at Christmastime and Tony sang *Lily The Pink*, and there were a lot of actions as he sung, and bobbing up and down. He entertained us that night.

We often talk about when Tony did *Lily The Pink*.

He isn't a good singer but he is a trier, and it was only for the comedy value anyway. He was always the joker of the family and always ready for a laugh.

But he took his football very seriously.

After he went semi-professional with Buxton in the Cheshire League he then signed for Blackburn, and he was really pleased to get the chance at Rovers. He lived in the pub across the road from Ewood Park, the Fox and Hounds, when he first signed, but he soon made Blackburn his home, with Eileen. Then Natalie arrived.

I tried to get to nearly every game when Tony signed for Blackburn. With me living in Sheffield, some of his away games were nearer for me than his home games, so I got to see a lot of those too.

I travelled to Blackburn lots of times and I always had someone from the family who wanted to come with me, or one or two of Tony's old pals that he had played with as an amateur.

His playing career came to an abrupt end when he broke his leg. Howard Kendall, who was manager at the time, was with him when I got to the hospital to see him.

It was a difficult time, but fortunately, Blackburn kept him involved and he started coaching.

His very good friend, Jack Walker looked after him really well, but he was successful in that role in his own right and, of course, managed the teams many times as caretaker.

I don't think he ever fancied the managerial job full-time. I think, in his mind, he thought if he takes the job full time and doesn't make a success of it he would have had to leave Blackburn, and that would be the worst possible thing that could happen to him.

Ultimately, when he did have to leave – not through his own choice – he took it hard.

He was quite happy doing the coaching and didn't have any ambitions to take it any further.

His strong reputation in that role went before him, and Blackburn fans love him.

I've never been anywhere in the world without bumping into someone who knows my brother.

Whenever I mentioned Tony's name to them and that I was his brother, I had a friend for life. That's happened all over Spain, the Canaries, Majorca… all the places I've been to.

And I've never heard anyone say a bad word against him.

Hilary Jarman
(Tony's youngest sister)

WE HAD A happy home at 39 Pipworth Road, and Tony was always tormenting and teasing us and doing things that made us laugh. He was a monkey.

There was one practical joke in particular I remember him

always playing, and he did it most Sundays. Even after we'd had a Sunday lunch, we still used to eat a meal in the evening and it was always salad with ham and things like that, and we always had tinned fruit with a can of cream that one of the boys had been given to shake, to thicken it up and then pour onto the fruit.

And every Sunday, Tony would pull his bowl full of fruit and cream to the end of the table and pretend it had dropped in his lap. And every time he did it, my mum reacted exactly the same, screaming… 'BE CAREFUL!' He used to do it all the time, sliding this bowl full of fruit and cream off the table and catching it.

My younger brother, Graham has a great sense of humour as well. He's a lot like Tony.

I don't know where it comes from. It certainly didn't come from my mum, that's for sure.

My dad was more light-hearted. He was a true gentleman, my dad.

He was a gentle man, very much like Tony. And Tony looks very much like my dad. As he's getting older, he's looking very much like my father.

Tony was just nice to be around; a very light-hearted person. This is why it's so tragic now, that Alzheimer's has taken that personality away.

Tony winning his race (top) while on holidays in Skegness, and (right) looking smart and ready for school. The Pipworth Road Secondary School football team (below) from 1959, with Tony centrestage

The Pipworth Road school team from 1960 (top) and, always the joker in the pack, Tony (back row, second from left) with the school team a year later

CHAPTER 2

Ups... and Downs

IN AN INTERVIEW, while he was still at Blackburn Rovers, Tony spoke of having vivid recollections of his first day at Ewood Park... walking along Nuttall Street, with the ground on one side, and a portakabin office opposite breaking up rows of red-bricked terraced housing.

He had arrived on trial at first, and met manager Eddie Quigley and played against Leeds reserves, before another trial match against Manchester United sealed the deal.

It was a big move, in every sense, leaving behind his home, his family and making the leap from semi-professional to full-time professional football.

Little could he have imagined then, on May 1, 1970 – just four days shy of his 21st birthday – that he would be at the club for as long as he was, undertaking as many roles as he did. But one thing that could be guaranteed is that he would put his heart and soul into whatever was asked of him, such was his approach to every task or challenge that he was faced with.

Tony had scored 33 goals in his last season at Buxton, and while it was his goalscoring feats that had initially caught Rovers' eye, after crossing the Pennines he was to be moulded into a workmanlike midfielder at Ewood Park.

He had joined a club experiencing troubled times.

There was a change of manager with Quigley being replaced by Johnny Carey mid-season. But it did not stop the slide and Rovers were relegated in Tony's first year, dropping into the Third Division for the first time in the club's history. Ken Furphy replaced Carey in the summer of 1971 and Tony had to fight for first team recognition.

◄◄◄ • ►►►

Ron Parkes

IN HIS EARLY days he was a little bit in and out of the team, when he first started.

One day he came home and he wasn't playing and I said, 'Do you feel like packing it in when you can't get in the team?'

And he said, 'Look, I love this job and I don't want to make any rash decisions because I really want to try to make it work. I love it so much. So I'm going to stick it out and try to get in the team on a regular basis'. It wasn't long after that he was the first name on the team-sheet every week.

And once he got established, he never got dropped again.

◄◄◄ • ►►►

OVER THE COURSE of time, Furphy realised that Parkes was the fulcrum; the one doing the vital leg work in midfield that so often goes un-noticed and under-appreciated, and towards the end of the 1972–73 season he had established himself in the starting XI.

It was not until the arrival of Gordon Lee as manager in January 1974, though, that there was true recognition of Tony's importance to the team.

A grafter, Tony was the type of player whom Lee rated highly, resulting in him playing a vital role in the 1974–75 Third Division championship campaign.

Tony was, like any good Yorkshireman, terrier-like, snapping at opponents' heals, closing down, winning the ball back, paramount to possession.

He plugged the gaps in midfield when Stuart Metcalfe pushed on and posed problems for opposition defences.

But while he was industrious and worked hard in the engine room, his eye for goal had not deserted him, and his non-stop energy could often lead to him bursting into the penalty box and chipping in with key goals.

By adding Ken Beamish, Graham Oates and Graham Hawkins to complement Tony and Metcalfe, Lee found a winning combination.

But a team on the up were soon brought back down to earth. Lee left for Newcastle United, and it was not the only loss as the club found themselves £221,000 in the red.

Jim Smith was appointed as Lee's successor, and despite injuries and no funds to strengthen the squad, they managed to stave off relegation that year.

But, after the managerial hotseat changed hands twice, the drop could not be avoided and at the end of the 1978–79 season Rovers found themselves relegated with four games to go.

On the plus side, Rovers had managed to reduce their debts, which allowed the club to rebuild and plot a successful promotion push under player-manager Howard Kendall, who as the driving force in midfield, received tremendous support from Tony.

◄◄◄ • ►►►

Derek Fazackerley
(Tony's teammate, colleague and friend, Blackburn Rovers 1969-86)

I REMEMBER TONY coming to Blackburn and signing as a striker from Buxton back in 1970, so we go back a long way. A very long way.

It was a big move for him coming from non-league football to what was then a Division Three side, but at the same time he showed his versatility because he came in as a striker and then moved back into midfield.

He made such a successful job as a midfield player, because in that role he was in the side that won promotion in 1974-75 with Gordon Lee's team.

He was a key part of the dressing-room, no doubt about it.

You knew what you were going to get out of him week-in, week-out. He was a very consistent performer, not spectacular by any means, but he would give you everything and he did a great job for the team.

He was a great character in the dressing-room too, well respected and well-liked by the rest of the players. An all-round good person really.

And he was a motivator.

He was one who, after a poor defeat or something like that, wasn't down for long and he was able to lift the spirits of the people around him, realising that as a professional these sort of things happen and you've got to get on and look forward to the next game and, hopefully, get a result that gets you going again.

◄◄◄ • ►►►

ALONGSIDE FAZACKERLEY, AS well as motivators, the two operated as mentors and role models to the youngsters who had been brought into the club to help climb up the league.

Simon Garner, who went on to be a club goalscoring legend, was among them.

◄◄◄ • ►►►

Simon Garner

TONY WAS ONE of the senior players when I arrived at Blackburn as a teenager.

As a player, he worked for 90 minutes.

He wasn't a stand-out player, but every game, if you marked him out of 10, he was always at least a seven. He always put a shift in, always worked hard and he went under the radar a bit.

He ran all game, he was as fit as anything. Him and Derek Fazackerley – they were the two senior players when I turned professional and they could train all day.

When I first started out at 18 or 19, when I was training with the first team, in the dressing-room Faz and Tony always had something to say and everyone listened. You could tell that those two, out of the whole room, were going to go into managment and coaching. They were the leaders in the dressing-room.

They were the two you would always think would carry on in football and be coaches, and obviously that's exactly what happened in the end. You'd come in after a game, and win or lose the manager would come in and say what he had to say and those two would always have an opinion too.

Tony would have an opinion about what we'd done well and what we'd done wrong.

That would be after a game.

And then, if we had a team meeting on the Monday, they'd have their say again. They were the main two speakers in the room.

That was impressionable for me as a young player. Starting off as a young kid, training with the first team, you look up to people like that.

He never tried to get me to stop smoking, though.

He wasn't a big drinker, and obviously he wasn't a smoker. But I think, like most managers in my career, they didn't try to stop me smoking, they just let me get on with it.

They took me as they found me.

◄◄◄ • ▶▶▶

A NEW DECADE brought a new start for Blackburn Rovers, as they secured promotion back to the second tier in the penultimate game of the 1979-80 season, and never looked back.

By this time, Tony was among the senior members in the squad and had already demonstrated all the qualities that would make him a good coach with the guidance that he was giving to the young, up and coming professionals – and he had been given some coaching responsibilities with some of the younger players too.

He was an almost ever-present in that promotion season; he trained impeccably well and expected others to mirror his exacting standards.

Teammates held him in high regard, and they knew that if they were ever in trouble on the ball, they just needed to get it to Tony and he would bail them out.

If others were having an off-day, Tony would work ever harder to compensate. But he was as impressionable off the pitch, as a person, as he was on it as a player.

◄◄◄ • ►►►

Mick Rathbone
(Blackburn Rovers, 1979-87)

TONY LOOKED AFTER me when I first got to Blackburn.

It was 1979. I'd arrived from Birmingham, on loan at first, before the move was made permanent.

I was probably only 19 or 20 when I arrived, and Tony would have been maybe 28 or 29. He was a senior player in the team and was really good to me; put me under his wing.

I was in a hotel called the Woodlands from March to the end of that season and had no car, and Tony would take me back after training.

He had a blue Capri, I think.

Many times he said, 'I'll drop you at the lights,' but he always took me the extra mile home up the big hill in Blackburn.

But that was Tony, always going the extra mile for people.

He's a very fine guy.

He was a really good player, good technically, gave everything all the time in training. He was a model professional, a lovely, *lovely* guy, very popular with all the players, and a bit of a father figure for me in those early days, alongside Faz.

I think he come into the game relatively late.

Perhaps that made him appreciate it all the more. He put everything in, applied himself really well.

He was ever the pro.

It was a massive drinking culture in those days in the 80s. It was all about how much you could drink between games, and Parkesy was one who, when we had the Christmas do, he'd have half a pint and he'd always say, 'Come on lads, we're not plumbers, we're not joiners... we're professional sports people, we should be drinking halves'. We shouldn't have been drinking at all, but his argument was that we should have been drinking just halves.

We had a few the night we won promotion from the Third Division, in the penultimate game of the 1979-80 season.

We clinched it against Bury on a Tuesday night. We were losing 1-0 at half-time and we went on to win 2-1. That feeling after winning with a game to spare… and we were at home to Bury the following Saturday.

Everybody piled into The Boar's Head pub when we got back from Bury – the players, their wives, *everybody*. A lot of players go through their career without really having much to celebrate and that was my first big celebration. A massive drink-up.

Howard Kendall was holding court… the pressure's off, everyone was together. Every time I go past that building, which is now a Co-op, it brings back memories of that night.

Most of your best times are tinged with sheer relief that it's over.

It's euphoria, but it's borne out of sheer relief.

Tony and Faz were key to it all, senior players like them – albeit only in their late-twenties themselves. (The idea of what constituted a senior player in those days!!). Him and Faz were so good. We had quite a few young players in the team, me and Garns – both early twenties – and a few others as well.

Running out at Bury that Tuesday night… if you win, it's glory!

But I'm a very negative person, so I'm thinking *If we lose there are 3,000 Rovers fans here…* so at that final whistle, you're either, metaphorically speaking, shoulder high, or it's a bad result and you need to win Saturday, or we've basically stuffed it all up.

There's always *that* threat.

But all was well that ended well… we're heroes, back in the pub.

But when we were out, Tony, as I say, would be drinking halves and he'd encourage us to do the same. So we started drinking halves, but twice as many of them, obviously.

And we all got a £20-a-week pay rise, which was what it was. I don't think we got any extra bonus. You got one for winning games and we obviously won a few, but I don't remember getting a bonus for going up.

We all went to Magaluf though, on the club, and had a great time.

We got there... and straight on the beach. Sun protection factor 50? Forget it. Nothing. Out.

We went in the bar at about two in the afternoon, in the sun. There was a slatted window in front of us and on the night four or five of us had slatted sun tans.

We had striped tans where the sun had gone through the blinds and caught us at an angle.

We had such a laugh out there all together.

Tony used to have this fantastic joke. My wife used to laugh her head off at it. What he'd do, he'd get a cup of tea and leave the spoon in it and he'd say, 'I'm going to have to stop drinking tea because every time I do, I get a pain in my eye,'.... and then he'd drink his tea and the spoon would go in his eye.

He was always the joker of the pack.

Such a great fella.

The Arbourthorne community team in Sheffield (top), and Tony getting a finishing touch for Rovers (below)

The Blackburn squad enjoying themselves after one training session (above) under the supervision of manager, Jim Smith. Tony and the lads get to meet the Iron Lady herself, Prime Minister Margaret Thatcher

CHAPTER 3

The Beginning of the End, and a new Beginning

THERE WERE MANY strings to Tony Parkes' bow.

◄◄◄ • ►►►

Derek Fazackerley

HE WASN'T JUST a good footballer. He qualified as a tiler before he came into full-time professional football, so when he was playing for Buxton he would have a job as well.

He brought those skills to the club, as we soon found out!

I can't remember him doing any jobs at the club, but he tiled my kitchen floor. He was quite cheap too! He used to do a little bit at the time, if you needed something like that doing.

◄◄◄ • ►►►

BUT FOOTBALL WAS Tony's forte, and all that knowledge of the game and skills in relaying information and instructions, came to the fore when injury – a nasty leg break – forced him into early retirement.

◄◄◄ ● ►►►

Mick Rathbone

MY LONG-TERM MEMORIES of Tony are fantastic. Although there is one bad one...

I don't know if anybody even knows this, but I gave him the pass that kind of finished his career, unfortunately. We were playing Wrexham at home in 1980 and I was playing left-back and Tony was playing on the left wing... and I gave him a bit of a short ball and the lad went through him.

He got a broken leg which finished his career.

It's not a secret now I've said that.

Other than that, I have really good memories of Tony. He made the move into coaching after that, and he always set a great example to the lads.

If you see that your coach is enthusiastic and, even though it's raining down Witton Park, he's up for it, that's important for a player.

He was first out, he'd be last in... and he'd do his press-ups and sit-ups, and he could do more than you... it was inspirational, and he led by example. That was Tony.

He was really fit. In those days we trained in the big park in

Blackburn, Witton Park, and every day before training in the warm-up, Parkesy would say, 'Right... GO!' And we'd run for about two miles through the park, at Tony's pace, and stop for a stretch by the water.

◄◄◄ • ►►►

AT THAT TIME, it was not just the injury that Tony had to contend with. It brought with it a health scare.

His daughter, Natalie, was a baby at the time so has no recollections of her own, but it is a story that she is familiar with.

◄◄◄ • ►►►

Natalie Parkes

THERE IS SO much about my dad's life that I didn't see, because he'd go to work and be that 'other person'.

I was 12 months old when he broke his leg and had to stop playing, so I don't remember that era at all, but it's something my mum and dad spoke about quite often, so I know a lot about it.

They brought him home from the hospital and dropped him straight off on the settee, but then he was back in hospital 24 hours later with a blood clot in his lung.

Obviously, now they mobilise patients, they put the sports cast on and all the rest of it. He was just lucky that my mum noticed that something was quite badly wrong.

He was still on the settee, because where we lived, on Livesey

Branch Road, the house was two-storey and he couldn't get him upstairs.

My mum said he was just ill, and it wasn't just pain, he wasn't right. So she rang for the ambulance, who initially said, 'Well, he's just had an operation… blah blah blah,' but she said this is not right, so they took him back into hospital.

And they got there just in time because the clot was entering his lung. If it had gone in there, I think it would have been game over.

He'd been struggling breathing. He was complaining of the pain, but not in his leg. After it had healed, he tried to get back playing but it just didn't work.

Fortunately, Rovers kept him on and gave him the coaching job.

◄◄◄ • ►►►

Simon Garner

IT SOUNDS AWFUL to say this, but when Tony suffered his broken leg, that gave me my chance in the team and it kicked my career off.

Obviously, Tony had played in midfield and I went in as a striker so there must have been some shuffling around. But I went straight in the team the week after Tony was injured.

We didn't have a massive squad in those days. Perhaps I was the last person they could call on!

For Tony, the injury put him onto the path of a career in

coaching, and it was one that he took to seamlessly.

He knew the players, he knew what they were like and he knew which ones needed an arm around them and to have a chat, and I'm sure, behind closed doors, he must have told a few players off as well. But he always did it in the right way.

He was destined to stay in the game.

He was so measured. The season after we were relegated from the Second Division we bounced straight back up and the likes of Tony kept us on an even keel to make sure we achieved that. He would never get too high with the highs or too low with the lows, he just went about his business and he was a great example.

Tony never used to raise his voice, never used to shout at you.

Whether he was playing or coaching, or when he was caretaker, he never used to lose his temper or anything like that. He was very calm about everything and precise and to the point. He'd turn round and say, 'Why didn't you do this or why didn't you do that?'

He didn't give you a rollicking.

It's quite an unusual temperament in football – or any competitive environment – but Tony was always very calm. And he got on well with the players.

I think the toughest thing for an ex-player is making that crossover into coaching or management when it involves players who have been your teammates. You've got to shut yourself off from them. You've got decisions to make, and Tony would always make the decisions and explain it to you. He was good at that.

Jim Smith was my first manager at Blackburn, when I was an apprentice, and they were a complete contrast.

There were quite a few transitional periods for Tony over the years. I'll give the club their dues, they always kept him on, and I think the managers who came in realised what he could do for the football club as well.

Tony was part and parcel of the club.

◄◄◄ • ►►►

IT WAS HARD for Tony to come to terms with an abrupt end to his playing career. But what softened the blow was the opportunity to stay in football, and significantly to stay at his beloved Blackburn Rovers. As one door closed, another one opened and, in 1980, a career in coaching began.

Tony was the epitome of a safe pair of hands. As a player he would have fulfilled any role had he been asked to, and he was no different as a coach.

He would 'muck in' with everything.

Quite literally, as it happened.

◄◄◄ • ►►►

Jim Furnell
(Blackburn Rovers coach, 1981-98)

I CAME TO Ewood with Bob Saxton in 1981, from Plymouth Argyle, and one of the stipulations from the chairman, Bill Fox, was that Tony stayed on the coaching staff. So he worked with Bob and the first team squad and I took the reserves and the youths.

Bob was the boss so what he said went. But we all just got along and worked really well together.

Tony was smashing. He was dedicated, keen and loved his football. You live and breathe football when you have been in it all your life and Tony was no different. But just generally speaking he was a 'What you see is what you get' type of person. No airs or graces. He was just steady and straightforward, and just got on with the job. He'd had a good playing career with the club before myself and Bob arrived, so that contributed to him earning the respect of the players. He tried to convey what he could do as a player into those he was coaching.

We'd nothing then, as a club. We didn't have two ha'pennies to rub together. We just all got on with the job, whatever needed doing. Even driving the bloody minibus everywhere. Both of us did that.

I remember once we drove down to Pleasington for training and Tony pulled up at the electrical shop by the Fox and Hounds. I said, 'Where are you going now?'

'We need some tape for the goals,' he replied. That's how bad it was.

But we all mucked in together, quite literally as it happened. Because another job we had to do – something else we did together – was get the dog muck off the pitches before the players came down.

That was after we'd actually found somewhere to play, of course.

We usually made a phone call at about 10 past nine in the morning to the parks' people at Pleasington to see if we could get a pitch.

Sometimes they'd say, 'You can have an area today,' so we had to take portable goals down there on those occasions. It wasn't ideal, but we just got on with it.

But wherever we were given to play, the players never saw us picking up the dog muck. They never saw any of that. By the time they got down there it was all nice and clear.

But Tony did it all with enthusiasm. Even *that*! He was great.

If we couldn't go to Pleasington for whatever reason, we went to a school down Heys Lane, or an all-weather pitch up Shadsworth. If we were indoors, we went to the YMCA, the gymnasium, anywhere we could get.

We had no money. We were skint.

But what we lacked in finances we made up for with friendships. We were a big family club and Tony was a constant.

He took over first team duties when Bob left in March 1986. The team played Portsmouth at home and we thought, 'We'll get battered here!' but Tony and the team got a victory. He did well. He was a safe pair of hands, was Tony.

I helped him out with the first team until Don Mackay came in as the new manager, but I still took the youth team when the first team had a game, so Tony was on his own.

He had the confidence and backing of the players, though. They didn't take the Mick, they got on with it… just like Tony always did.

I think all the players he worked with owe him a great debt.

◄◄◄ ● ►►►

MARK ATKINS WOULD certainly concur with that sentiment.

Everyone who worked with Tony took something from the experience, but some more than others.

As far as Atkins was concerned, coming under his tutelage was career defining.

For starters, Tony was behind his move to Ewood Park. He arrived for a modest £45,000 after Tony had scouted him at Scunthorpe, and subsequently recommended him to Don Mackay. Then, after Mackay's departure in September 1991, in calling the first team shots as caretaker, Tony put Atkins on a path that was to shape the rest of his playing days, and made him a Premier League winner as the only player to survive the Rovers revolution under Kenny Dalglish.

He credits Tony's influence in that, for initiating his own personal transformation.

◄◄◄ ● ►►►

Mark Atkins
(Blackburn Rovers 1988-95)

TONY WAS A big part of my career at Blackburn. He was the one who phoned me up to come for talks, and I ended up signing.

Don Mackay was manager in 1988 and Tony was assistant, and he'd been to look at me in a couple of games at Scunthorpe.

After getting the call. I came in the next day and basically just signed on the dot straight away… I loved the place that much, and Tony had a big say in it.

He was a nice guy and really knew his stuff football-wise,

getting involved in the training... and he was the fittest man at the club probably... fitter than all the players. He used to like his running, so the warm-ups were quite decent. Players were moaning like mad at the back though, but it was all good natured and all part and parcel of it.

As well as being assistant-manager, Tony was reserve team manager as well. It's not like it is now where clubs can carry huge staff. Very often back then, one person would have two jobs. At least!

The same went for the players sometimes too. Because we were young players, in the late 80s you'd be asked to play in the reserves as well as the first team, if they were short of players. I played a couple of reserve games in midfield and I think that's probably when Tony saw what I could do, and straightaway when he got the caretaker role he moved me into midfield.

I hadn't thought about it at the time but it became my preferred position, and from then on my career went up and up.

When I looked at the board when Tony named the team, I thought *That can't be my name...* but it was.

It was a masterstroke. He spotted that I could do a job in there and it was a case of not seeing how it goes; he had enough faith in me to put me in there and say, 'That's going to be your position'.

I owe him a great debt in my career because I went on from there and that really launched me onto a different level. To win a Premiership medal after that was fantastic, and obviously Tony was involved and instrumental in that as well.

But as well as a great coach, he was just great to be around.

He liked a joke and could get involved in things. I think sometimes he got the brunt of it as well, but he could take it as well as give it, and you knew when you had to stop with him.

He was the go-to for players, if they needed to discuss anything.

Any time you needed any help, he was the one you would go to.

When he became caretaker manager, you knew he could do a good job just because of how he was as a player and as assistant-manager.

He had the respect of the club.

The Rovers squad celebrate promotion to Division 2 at the end of the 1974-75 season and (below) Tony and Duncan McKenzie enjoy that winning feeling in the dressing-room

Tony being carried off at Ewood Park after breaking his leg against Wrexham (right), and still feeling the pain (below)

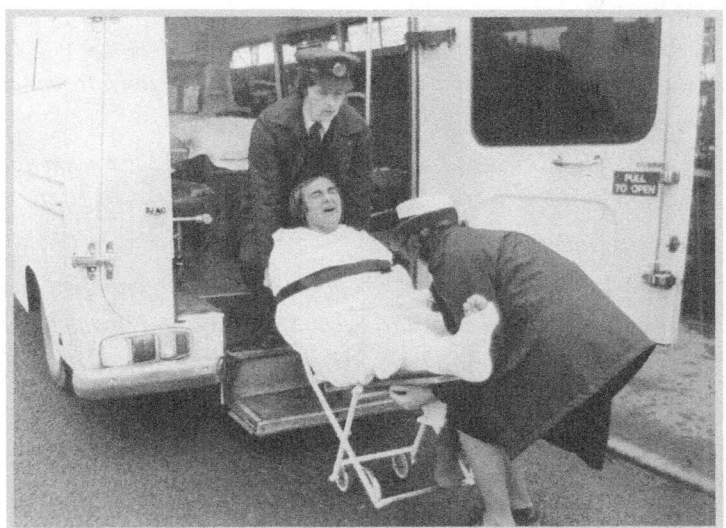

CHAPTER 4

A new Niche... and a Trophy!

THE PERIOD IN between Bobby Saxton's departure and Don Mackay's arrival provided Tony with his first real taste of management.

Some might have been daunted at the prospect of taking charge of first team duties, even on a temporary basis. But not Tony. It was as if he revelled in it.

Yet, while he enjoyed the decision making, he did not want the responsibility of it — and everything that came with the role of manager... full-time.

But even in the short-term it required a level of organisation and discipline and, in all honesty, it astounded Eileen and Natalie that he proved a dab hand with both, albeit only when it came to football.

◄◄◄ • ►►►

Natalie Parkes

I ALWAYS USED to laugh and say, 'How can you discipline these players? You'd be rubbish at that'. Because at home it was my mum who wore the trousers and my dad just went along with it.

Even though my mum would often say, 'Wait til' your dad gets home' it was her I was scared of.

It was my mum who would discipline at home, but I think at the football, how dad must have carried himself, he always had that respect.

I think he expected so much of the team, it was that sense of, 'If you fail to deliver, you're disappointing me', and that's the worst thing anyone can say to you... you're not mad with them, you're not angry with them, they're not driving you crazy... but you're disappointed.

My dad couldn't organise a thing, never has been able to, but he'd be the one who had all the passports when they went on pre-season.

It's funny, that... because he was not the best of travellers himself.

Far from it.

On holiday my dad always insisted we'd have a pedalo, but he'd go green and be sick. Every year, no matter where we were.

Motion sickness... he's not good.

When we went to Florida for the first time, he'd have to go on rides with me and he'd be green. I would have been 14.

We went on a parachute ride that went up a bit and floated down and he had to go and get their version of paracetamol to settle down. He never liked flying, and if the plane had propellers, which a lot of them did if the team was playing away at Southampton or somewhere, he dreaded it. But I think in front of the players and staff he just learned to mask it.

On the coach, he wasn't as bad if he could sit in a certain place. But on a plane his knuckles would go white, he'd hate it. If it hit turbulence, he was terrible.

That's probably the only time I've ever seen him lose control in a way.

So, yes, travelling wasn't great. But somehow he managed to organise an entire squad. He was in charge of all the keys. And it baffled me how he could do that, but he can't organise a thing at home.

But he knew the game, he knew what he was talking about and he knew his way around a dressing-room and how to handle one.

◄◄◄ • ►►►

THIS KNOW-HOW inspired a Rovers revival post-Saxton and put the team on the path to Wembley.

Blackburn Rovers had made football history with a hat-trick of FA Cup wins, but that was back in the 1800s.

Since achieving promotion back to the Second Division in 1980, they had got out of the habit of winning things. So when they earned a trip to Wembley for the Full Members' Cup final in March 1987, with passion for the club rekindled, 28,000 fans ventured to the capital to cheer them on.

Mackay had made an instant impact by securing a cup final in his first season. But it must not be forgotten that Tony had played a significant part in their progress. By the time the new manager had been installed, Rovers were in the last eight having beaten Huddersfield – under Bobby Saxton's watch – before Tony oversaw wins against Sheffield United and Oxford United.

Mackay was at the helm when they took on a Chelsea side that sat mid-table in the First Division, and Rovers won 3-0 at Ewood Park, with Sean Curry, who Tony had signed from Liverpool in his capacity as caretaker, on the scoresheet, along with Simon Garner and Ian Miller.

Ipswich stood in the way of them and the final, but not for long as Rovers secured a comfortable 3-0 home win to set up a meeting with First Division Charlton Athletic beneath the Twin Towers.

Colin Hendry, who made his debut against Ipswich, had been signed as a young defender but Mackay had observed some attacking qualities, and Hendry unleashed them with the winning goal five minutes from time – the only goal – to make Rovers' first Wembley cup final since 1960 an even more memorable occasion.

◄◄◄ ● ►►►

Colin Hendry
(Blackburn Rovers 1987-89, 1991-98)

THE FULL MEMBERS' Cup final. What a day that was!

Winning that… how big it was, and how important it was to the football club. And I was lucky enough to score a goal in a cup final at Wembley. It's something Tony and I often talked about whenever we saw each other years later.

Simon Garner

IT WAS A brilliant time and one that Tony really enjoyed as well.

The week beforehand, the whole build-up to it and then the day itself. Winning the game was absolutely brilliant... to win at Wembley.

And then the town came out to celebrate with us the night after. Such a special occasion.

◄◄◄ • ►►►

ROVERS WENT ON to win much bigger and better things than the Full Members' Cup, but Tony Parkes would never downplay the significance of that day.

*Young and in love:
Tony and Eileen on
holidays in the 60s
(right), and on their
wedding day, June
28, 1974*

Mr Blackburn Rovers: Tony at Nuttall St, Ewood Park

CHAPTER 5

Play-off Heartache

IF EVER EVIDENCE was needed that Tony Parkes put the 'care' into caretaker, it came after Rovers' Division Two play-off final defeat to Crystal Palace.

It was 1989.

Twelve months earlier, they had been comprehensively beaten by Chelsea over a two-legged semi-final, 3-0 on aggregate.

This time, by the narrowest of margins, they had managed to go one step further. After a goalless draw against Watford at Ewood Park, Simon Garner put them in front in the re-match at Vicarage Road. Neil Redfearn equalised for the Hornets, but Rovers progressed by virtue of the away goals' rule.

These days, the play-off finals are staged at Wembley Stadium, but back then it followed the same format as the semis and was a two-legged affair.

Rovers, taking on a Crystal Palace side that had celebrated a 3-0 aggregate win over Swindon, took a two-goal advantage to Selhurst Park courtesy of a 3-1 win at Ewood Park.

But Ian Wright scored twice as Palace overhauled the deficit. His second, late in extra time, made it 4-3 and Palace fans poured onto the pitch in their thousands.

Rovers had been within touching distance of a long awaited return to the First Division, but had somehow lost their grip.

In the silence of the shower room, tears streamed down Tony's face.

◄◄◄ • ►►►

Colin Hendry

I WAS THE only other one there. He started crying.

I've only ever seen two grown men cry after a game… one was Tony, the other was Gary McAllister after Euro '96 when he missed a penalty.

At the end of the day, it's just a game of football. But for Tony, he had been at Blackburn all his career and he had got to the brink of the top division.

It was all just too much.

I had never seen that before in football. It was so poignant and very humbling to see a man brought up in football, a football coach, show his emotions like that.

He had enough about him to feel so much love and affection for the club that that's what it did to him.

I told him that we would come back and try to get there again.

But at the time, he must have felt like that *was it.* Our best chance had gone. We weren't a big city club. It was a long shot to get that far and challenge again.

I'm sure the scenes at the end of the game must have had something to do with how emotionally charged he was as well.

The Palace fans were on the side of the pitch.

George Courtney was the referee that day. He should have called the game off against Crystal Palace. The crowd were on the side of the pitch, the game should have been stopped. It was absolute carnage.

Ironically, he then refereed our play-off final at Wembley with Leicester in '92, so we all eventually made amends.

That felt a long way off at the time though, especially to Tony. Nobody could have foreseen what was to come a few years later, I expect. Least of all him, because he'd been at the club in some really tough times, so it would have been hard to envisage the level of achievement the club went on to enjoy... the experiences we had.

Tony was a massive focal point in my career because I had moved from a completely different part of the world.

It was a big enough jump for me to move from my hometown of Keith, in Scotland, to Dundee. I was a farming, out-back type personality. Moving from there to England, it was a complete change for me. But Tony was always there to help. He always made you smile.

He always had a dry sense of humour and his banter was brilliant.

When I first came in 1987, he was really fit. He did the pre-season with us. I was 21 and he was up with us at the front, keeping up with us. It was mad. He was *super* fit.

He had a bit of everything.

Mr Blackburn Rovers is probably as accurate a description of him as anyone could have. I don't believe for a minute there's anything he couldn't have turned his hand to, any role or job within the football club.

And he worked with so many different managers, all with different characters, and he adapted to every situation, which tells you how easy going he is and how professional he was.

And for the players, he was a brilliant buffer between us and whoever was in charge. Having people to listen to you was really important.

Tony was always very good at that, not just about football but life in general, and things that happen.

He is, and has been, not just a coach and figurehead in and around, but a bit of a counsellor. He wouldn't give his opinion right away either, which was always noticeable.

He would probably always answer a question given to him with a question back.

We had a good post-mortem after every game. If someone was to go to him and say, 'Were we really that bad at West Ham?', for example, he would say, 'Did you feel you played well?'

He would come back at you with a question and get into a conversation with you and try to eke out values from the discussion.

From that, I would go and walk my dogs and figure things out on my own, analyse and think about things on my own and take on board what people say and put it to good use the next time you play.

It was good psychology.

◄◄◄ • ►►►

THE PLAY-OFFS were proving to be more of a curse than a blessing as Rovers missed out again the season after, but this time at the semi-final stage once more – losing 2-1 in both legs against Swindon Town. Tony must have felt they were always destined to be the bridesmaid and never the bride. Third time unlucky.

Even more frustratingly, the 1990-91 season – in comparison – was a flop.

But then, in rode the club's knight in shining armour, Jack Walker, and Blackburn Rovers underwent a transformation that was to ultimately transform football... and football business.

Tony took caretaker charge for the second time, after Don Mackay was sacked just a few games into the 1991-92 season.

Walker, affectionately nicknamed 'Uncle Jack' by supporters, had already proved he had meant business by making not one, but two bids to Tottenham Hotspur for Gary Lineker – the second for a cool £1million. Attempts to sign Teddy Sheringham had been met with ridicule amongst the media, but that did not bother Walker, who had no qualms about approaching Kenny Dalglish about the vacant post at Ewood Park.

The pressures of being in charge of a club like Liverpool had led to Dalglish resigning in February 1991, but he was soon bitten by the football bug again, and enticed by the Ewood ambition.

There were conversations going on behind the scenes but, in the meantime, Tony not only steadied the ship but started to steer it in the right direction.

Rovers won away at Derby County, drew 1-1 at Sunderland, and recorded home wins against Port Vale and Watford, to climb away from the relegation zone.

They lost at Leicester, drew 0-0 at home to Tranmere, but then bounced back with a 3-1 win at Millwall to climb into the top half of the table for the first time in over a year.

A new era was dawning.

Dalglish and his assistant, Ray Harford, were at the next game, against Plymouth Argyle at Ewood Park.

They went into the home dressing-room to meet the players before kick-off, shaking each of them by the hand and wishing them well for the upcoming 90 minutes for which, having picked the team, Tony remained in charge.

Before Dalglish and Harford took their seats in the Nuttall Street Stand, Walker formally introduced the new management duo to the media, who were keen to learn what had brought them to Blackburn Rovers.

'When I left Anfield, I was in need of a rest,' Dalglish told them. 'I had had enough, and I needed to get away and recharge my batteries. Now they've been recharged and I'm looking forward to getting back to work.

'I was enjoying the way of life. I was enjoying being a normal person, but the missus wanted me out of the house, she told me to get a job!'

He had been sold a dream of being a force in the First Division. Jack Walker had set out a five-year plan to achieve it.

Dalglish and Harford had signed up to the first three years of that vision, and after taking their seats in the stand, they watched Tony Parkes continue to lay the platform to achieve it.

◄◄◄ • ►►►

Simon Garner

TONY ALWAYS DID a good job when he took on the caretaker manager role, and he did it a few times when I was playing.

We played Plymouth at home in his last game in charge, before Kenny Dalglish took over.

Tony had picked the team, Dalglish was sitting in the directors' box. You're trying to impress the new manager, knowing he's watching.

I scored two goals in a 5-2 win and I thought *I'll be all right for next week*, but obviously I didn't impress him enough... and Dalglish dropped me.

◄◄◄ • ►►►

STEVE LIVINGSTONE REPLACED Garner in the line-up as one of three changes for Dalglish's first game in charge, away to Swindon.

It wasn't the dream start, as Rovers lost 2-1.

But with Tony as an ally, progress was quickly made, both on and off the field with an influx of new signings, including a familiar face with the return of Colin Hendry, two years after he had left for Manchester City.

Mike Newell arrived too as a £1.1million club record signing from Everton, and Gordon Cowans brought bags of experience from Aston Villa.

The promotion push had started in earnest, and Tony was in the thick of it all.

Indeed, he was integral to it.

*Tony and Natalie at home on Livesey Branch Road in July, 1981
(top), and happy on holidays (below)... June, 1983*

Tony, Eileen and Natalie... in Majorca, June, 1984

CHAPTER 6

Rovers' Revolution

DURING TALKS WITH Jack Walker and Rovers' chairman, Bill Fox, Kenny Dalglish had asked for Ray Harford to be recruited as his number two.

Harford was manager of Wimbledon at the time, but had given notice of his resignation. His reputation as a coach, which included a League Cup winners' medal with Luton, was second to none.

Dalglish made one other stipulation to the board as well…

◄◄◄ • ►►►

Sir Kenny Dalglish
(Blackburn Rovers, October 1991-June 1995)

BLACKBURN APPROACHED ME to take the job and my first conversation was, 'I'll take the job if Tony Parkes is staying'.

If Tony hadn't have stayed then I wouldn't have gone.

I didn't know him very well, I just knew what he was like in the profession that he worked in. I knew what he meant to Blackburn, and his integrity was brilliant, so there were no problems.

He was obviously going to be a great help to myself, he knew the players really well, he knew the club really well, and he knew his way round about the club, which I felt was really important.

It was the 1991-92 season.

The manager had got the sack after a month and Tony took caretaker charge. He took them up a few places in the league, I think they were second bottom and Tony took them up to somewhere roundabout mid-table.

◄◄◄ • ►►►

ROVERS EVENTUALLY FINISHED sixth, winning a three-way race for the final play-off spot on the last day of the season, courtesy of an away win at Plymouth, who needed the points to survive.

It epitomised what had been a dramatic season, with a big-name manager and some big signings.

And in typical Rovers fashion the play-off process was anything but straightforward.

In their semi-final with Derby County, the Rams raced into a 2-0 lead in the first leg at Ewood. Tony must have shuddered at the thought of the ghosts of play-offs past coming back to haunt them. But they fought back to go into the break level at 2-2, before David Speedie scored twice in the second half to make it 4-2.

Derby fans turned the Baseball Ground into a cauldron of noise for the second leg. They scored first. Kevin Moran equalised, but then the Rams led 2-1, making it 5-4 on aggregate. Had they got a third, the away goals' rule would have favoured them. But Rovers held on and made it to Wembley, which – as well as earning promotion via the penalty spot against Leicester City – proved to be an extra special occasion for Tony.

◄◄◄ • ►►►

Sir Kenny Dalglish

WHEN WE GOT to the play-off final at Wembley, the manager leads the team out, and I said to Tony, 'You do it. You lead the team out at Wembley'.

He was stuck a wee bit in his throat.

It stuck in everybody's throat, anybody who had anything to do with Blackburn, but that's an indication of how important he was and how appreciative we were for all the work that he'd done.

It was important for me to show my appreciation on behalf of everybody who had anything to do with, or any feeling towards, Blackburn. They would have loved it and recognised it as well.

Natalie Parkes

HE FOUND OUT about it the day before. Kenny said to him, 'It's your team… I haven't been here long enough'.

It was a proud day. A really special day for him… for all of us.

Apart from the suit they put him in. They were awful suits.

They were designer suits, but none of them fit. They were all too big. And they were pale as well, but Kenny had picked the colour.

Apart from that, it was the perfect day.

I think that's what made that era.

There was the respect there. Everyone respected Kenny with what he'd achieved, but that didn't go to his head. He knew he needed people around him.

Ray had certain skills, my dad had certain skills and they all bounced off each other.

Colin Hendry

WHEN YOU LOOK back to winning the promotion, between Kenny, Ray and Tony, you had three so very different characters, but they all helped you in a certain way.

Having been with Tony at the time of leaving Blackburn, he said to me he wasn't sure signing for Manchester City was the right thing for me to do. But it was, and I came back a better footballer, and Tony recognised that.

He was quick to notice things.

They all had their own different qualities and they all worked so well together, and because of that we had a lot of great times.

◄◄◄ • ►►►

SPEAK TO ANYONE who knows Tony – his relatives, his former teammates, ex-colleagues and former managers – and you will get a consistent theme...

Loyal.

Hard-working.

Trustworthy.

Caring.

Funny.

Tony Parkes is all of the above, and more.

These are qualities that he has carried throughout his life, as a son, brother, husband, dad and grandad.

And these are the qualities that made him a must when it came to Kenny Dalglish's backroom team.

With Tony a constant at Ewood Park for over two decades at the time of Dalglish's appointment in 1991, it was a relationship that the former Liverpool manager was not prepared to sever under any circumstances.

He had earmarked Ray Harford as his assistant-manager, but Tony was just as much part of the package for Dalglish. He insisted on it, in fact.

Forget the idea that three is a crowd, this trio was the perfect match.

◄◄◄ • ►►►

Sir Kenny Dalglish

WE ALL GOT on really well and worked so well together... myself, Tony and Ray. I think the important thing was, we each had respect for one other.

Tony or Ray gave their opinions and you would listen, and there was no problem with them giving their opinions. But at the end of the day, the manager makes the decisions and they accepted that .

They came up with some ideas and a lot of them were very good, so we would take them. But they also had to accept that not everything you say is good.

We all realised what our jobs were and nobody tried to take over anybody's job… they just knew what their job was and they did it. And Tony and Ray did a magnificent job.

Originally, Tony's role was to organise where we were training, because we never had a training ground until Brockhall was built, so that was first and foremost to get it up and running.

Before we went out, we would discuss various aspects of how we should be training and how we should be travelling to the games, what happened in the games before and what we do moving forward. Just preparation.

And everyone had their say in what we did.

He got involved in training too.

He was fitter than some of the players in fact. He looked after himself.

◄◄◄ • ►►►

BUT TONY'S PRIMARY role, of course, was to look after the players and help get them to the peak of their powers for an assault on the Premier League.

Rovers hit top spot in November and entered into a head-to-head battle with Manchester United, and by early April they had established an eight-point lead. But points were dropped over Easter, with a late draw at Leeds, followed by a shock home defeat to Manchester City two days later.

Calm was restored with a 2-1 home win over Crystal Palace later that week, but not for long, as Rovers went to West Ham United and lost again.

Rovers hosted Newcastle United in their final home game of the season, with Alan Shearer scoring against his boyhood club to secure a 1-0 win, as Tim Flowers made key saves at the other end to retain top spot.

Manchester United later beat Southampton to reduce the deficit to two points and send the championship race to a dramatic final day.

Rovers were at Anfield.

Manchester United were at West Ham, and favourites to get the win they needed.

Shearer fired Rovers in front, while West Ham took the lead in their game soon after. So far so good.

But John Barnes equalised for Liverpool on 64 minutes, just before United had drawn level at Upton Park.

Time stood still when Jamie Redknapp made it 2-1 with a free-kick in injury time. But news soon trickled through that the other game had ended all square, despite frantic late pressure by Alex Ferguson's men. Despite defeat, Rovers were winners.

Champions.

In the book They Think It's All Rovers – a variety of tales of Ewood, which was compiled to commemorate the club's 125th anniversary – Tony recounts being crowned champions of England at Anfield.

'The day we clinched the Premiership at Anfield was marvellous and I can remember every minute of it... not just the game but the build-up and the celebrations,' he said.

'All the people crammed into Anfield seemed to want us to win, in order to deny Manchester United. When Jamie Redknapp scored to put Liverpool ahead near the end everything threatened to go sour, but the cameramen situated next to our dug-out shouted across that it didn't matter, for United had only managed a draw... and the title was ours.

Kenny and Ray were dancing on the pitch and we were all joining in... it must have looked very strange as our game was still going on.

When we got back into the dressing-room, everyone was so happy.

Kenny hadn't allowed any talk of winning the league right up to the final day and so we hadn't been able to make any plans in advance.

We decided to try to gate-crash the Bistro French restaurant in Preston and the owner, Ian Boasman, welcomed us with open arms.

The place looked full when we got there, but somehow they managed to squeeze us in.

The Drifters were on, and it was quite a night.'

The images of Kenny Dalglish, Ray Harford and Tony Parkes united in celebration, with the trophy, are iconic.

◄◄◄ • ►►►

Sir Kenny Dalglish

TO WIN THE Premier League was a dream come true. Really. You wake up the next morning and you think it is a dream.

And it was a good night after we won.

Tony drank halves, aye, but he could drink a lot of them. Especially that night.

We enjoyed ourselves. We went to Bistro French in Preston, and everybody that we could fit in went. And to be fair, we never booked it until afterwards.

Players had their wives, their parents and friends there. As many as we could get in, we got in. It was a special evening.

It was a place where you could dance on the tables. I never saw Tony doing that. I think he was under them!

It was a 'pinch me' moment for everybody.

Everybody really enjoyed it, but I think it was a wee bit special for the likes of Tony, who had been at Blackburn for so long as a player and then on the coaching staff, taken over as caretaker manager and then coming in beside us to work on our backroom staff and do a fantastic job.

With him being that close to the club, it would have been special, not because it meant any less than that to us, but I think for people like Tony... it was a special occasion.

Eileen and Tony in Cockington, Torquay

*Silverware: Natalie and her dad testing out the Premiership trophy
together at Rovers' training ground in 1995*

CHAPTER 7

The Million Pound Men

EWOOD PARK WAS being redeveloped, a state-of-the-art training facility at Brockhall was being built, and big money was being spent on big players for Blackburn Rovers.

Five-figure sums were a thing of the past thanks to Jack Walker's millions as he looked to achieve his big and bold ambitions for his football club.

Club record transfer fees were being smashed left, right and centre; indeed British transfer records were broken, and with it came big personalities and Porsches as Rovers prepared for life in the Premier League. But not just to exist in it… to win it, and then after they had won it… to challenge again.

Post-promotion, Stuart Ripley had cost £1.2million from Middlesbrough one week, Alan Shearer £3.3m from Southampton another. Rovers finished fourth. That summer they spent £2.7m on signing Paul Warhurst from Sheffield Wednesday, a similar figure to *get David Batty from Leeds, and later £2m to secure goalkeeper Tim Flowers from Southampton. Money well spent.*

Rovers had finished second, enjoyed their most productive season in 99 years and earned a place in a European cup competition – the UEFA Cup – for the first time in the club's history.

Tony was not a good traveller, but he adapted, just as he did to the cash being splashed again as another new British transfer record was set with the capture of Chris Sutton from Norwich for £5m.

The SAS – Shearer and Sutton – was born and the jigsaw was pretty much complete.

Rovers had launched themselves into a different stratosphere to what this son of Sheffield was used to, but Tony took it all on board and helped mould a dressing-room packed with talented individuals into a team.

◄◄◄ ● ►►►

Alan Shearer
(Blackburn Rovers, 1992-96)

I MET TONY as soon as I'd signed for Blackburn in '92 and his warmth and his personality shone through straightaway.

We had Kenny and Ray at the forefront of the management team, but obviously Tony was a part of that as well, and from the minute I walked into the Blackburn dressing-room, it was pretty obvious how popular Tony was with all the players. And that, for me, was great.

The whole dressing-room made me feel at home.

Although I went over to Southport to live, it was still the dressing-room that made it easier for me to settle after moving from Southampton. It was a really warm and welcoming dressing-room, and Tony played a huge part in that.

His was always the first voice that we heard in a morning – that Yorkshire accent that everyone used to (excuse the language) take the p*** out of and shout... 'PARKESY trying to mimic him, which he didn't mind.

He loved a laugh and a joke, but you also knew he was a serious guy and how much he loved his football.

As I said, he was the first person we saw in the morning before training. He was the first person in the dressing-room. He'd be the one checking everyone was in on time, seeing what we were all laughing at, what we were up to...

One of Tony's jobs was the link between the dressing-room and the management; a hugely important job and one that he was great at. The lads absolutely loved him and loved his personality.

He looked after everyone. If you had any issues or you wanted to go and see the manager, it was always Tony that you'd go and see, and who you spoke to first. He would clear everything up.

He knew everyone inside out, he knew everyone's personality, he knew what made everyone tick... what people liked and what they didn't like, and that was what was good about him. He knew everyone really, *really* well.

And you could talk to him about anything. He was the first port of call, so you built a trust with him. And no one knew the club better than him, anyway – that's how everyone felt, because he'd been there for so long and he was so popular with everyone, you could speak to him about anything.

There probably aren't many that you could say that about.

Football's a brutal business, and dressing-rooms can be tough, and personalities often clash because of the nature of the sport but I can't remember anyone falling out with him and that's very unique and very rare in a dressing-room, because you're always going to get clashes; you're always going to get a difference of opinion or different personalities.

But there's not once I can remember someone falling out with him, which is very, *very* rare in the game.

His training sessions were very good.

He had a great rapport with Kenny and Ray.

Tony and Ray would put on most of the sessions, with Kenny joining in with them a lot as well.

Tony didn't mind joining in training, either. If he could take the Mick out of one or two then there's no doubt about it, he would do that. But training was our chance to get our own back on him, too. He didn't mind someone kicking him or letting him know they were there.

I imagine part of his job in the morning was to go and locate a piece of grass that we could go and train on in the first place, which is remarkable really.

For a team that won the Premiership within three years of promotion, for the first two years we didn't have a training ground! Amazing really.

And part of Tony's job was to go and sort all of that.

We didn't have a clue where we were going until we turned up on the day of training. But that wouldn't have fazed Tony.

Nothing did. Nothing bothered him.

We had some big personalities in our dressing-room, and he just took everything in his stride and got on with everyone.

And he had a lot to deal with. He had to deal with players being left out, he had to deal with players who weren't happy, but again that's what's sort of unique and what was different about our dressing-room, because it was his job to handle all that… and he did all that, and that's why everyone respected him.

It's a difficult job. To try to pick someone up who's been left out and then still get on with them is difficult. To be able to do that successfully, it was a sign of who and what he was.

He was a calming influence too.

The year we won the title, towards the end of the season we all got a bit nervy, Kenny included, and Kenny had been there, seen it and done it! We were all feeling the nerves, but we leaned on each other, and Tony in particular.

The more nervy we got, the more jokes he liked to tell. He was good at keeping us smiling, or at least trying to. He was definitely one of the jokers and we loved him.

To win the Premier League, or Premiership as it was then, you could see at the end against Liverpool there was just huge relief for all of us. But you could see, especially, what it meant to Tony.

He had been there for so long. He'd been there in the tough times, he was there at the play-off final at Wembley and when Blackburn came up into the Premier League. For him to go from where the club had been, to where we got to… it was an amazing achievement for us all, but for Tony to be a part of that after being at the club for so long, it was great to see.

Footballers, football people and dressing-rooms… when you leave a club you are ships that pass in the night, more often than not. There's not a great many that go from a dressing-room and keep in touch.

But so many of us have kept in touch with Tony, and that tells you everything about him, how great everyone thought he was and how respected he was by everyone.

I've seen him on the pitch at times in recent years with his daughter, Natalie, which is great to see and the club are doing their bit for him.

It would be wonderful if something was named after him – whatever it is it would be great, if something at the football club was named after him because he deserves it.

Tony is an amazing guy.

I really like him and I really respect him.

Regardless of football, he's a guy I would like and respect because of how he is as a person. But every football club needs a Tony Parkes, and if everyone was like Tony in football it would be a nicer game.

◄◄◄ ● ►►►

THE TROUBLE WITH hitting the heights is, there's only one way to go.

Kenny Dalglish had decided to call it a day. After all, how could the previous season ever be topped? So, six weeks after being crowned champions, there was a change of management, with Ray Harford taking the reins and Dalglish moving 'upstairs' to become Director of Football, meaning Tony was promoted once more to the role of assistant, while Derek Fazackerley returned to the club as first team coach after a spell at Newcastle United.

After struggling to look capable of defending their title and being slow to make signings, improvements began to be made on all fronts. Except in Europe.

Results were almost the least of their worries when David Batty and Graeme Le Saux came to blows on the pitch against Spartak Moscow. Something Tony had to deal with behind the scenes. But, ultimately, it triggered the break-up of the championship team at the end of the season and a seventh-place finish.

The club reluctantly sold Alan Shearer to Newcastle for £15 million, Mike Newell moved to Birmingham, Dalglish left, and by the end of October, with Rovers bottom without a league win at that point, Harford resigned.

Cometh the hour, cometh the man... and Tony once more triggered the revival. He kept his head down and got the job done while talk of Sven Goran Eriksson taking charge made the headlines.

In December, it was announced that Eriksson had agreed a three-year deal once his contract with Sampdoria had expired in the summer, and that Tony would remain in charge until then. But in February Eriksson did a U-turn and decided to stay in Italy.

Roy Hodgson of Inter Milan became 'Roy of the Rovers' that summer instead.

In the meantime, Tony was professionalism personified with his efforts in steering the club to a 13th place finish recognised by Jack Walker, who made a special presentation to the club stalwart and loyal servant before the last game of the season against Leicester, in recognition of his wonderful work with the squad.

And Tony was later presented with a Carling No.1 award, which was given to individuals who had made an outstanding contribution to the game.

There was little respite, with the manager's hotseat changing hands twice in two years – Hodgson lasted just over a year, Kidd just less than – until things stabilised with the arrival of Graeme Souness, another former Liverpool manager.

Rather than winning the Premier League, Souness was tasked with getting back there.

◄◄◄ • ►►►

Derek Fazackerley

WHENEVER THERE WAS a change of manager, Tony provided continuity. He was the constant.

(Derek Fazackerley worked alongside Tony to preserve Rovers' Premier League status amid a backdrop of managerial mayhem, before Hodgson's arrival in the summer of 1997)

The club knew they could rely on him and he stepped into the manager's shoes in a caretaker capacity on several occasions, quite successfully as well.

Would he have ever fancied being the manager himself? It's difficult.

Obviously, there was a time where it possibly could have happened, but I think when Jack Walker came into the club and there was that much money involved, it was always going to be a 'personality' to try to drive the club forward, particularly when you were trying to sign people like Alan Shearer and the side that was developed over that period of time.

They needed big personalities as a manager to attract those sorts of players. So in that respect, Tony was probably a little bit unlucky to miss out. But he shared in the success of that team and was a key part of the dynamic with Kenny Dalglish and Ray Harford, especially. He was an instrumental part of what went on around the football club at that particular time.

I'm not sure any of the managers would have known Tony beforehand, but he would have been recommended by the board as a good and loyal servant, and somebody who had the club at heart and somebody that could be trusted. Then it's up to the manager at that particular time, having worked for them for a short period, to make their mind up what they wanted to do, and of course they all kept him.

I left the club and came back. We had some good times together, Tony and I, as players and then when we both made the move into coaching.

But we didn't always have it easy, particularly when Kenny and Ray left and myself and Tony were left in charge before the arrival of Roy Hodgson. And that was a long season where we were struggling at times, and you needed each other. You have to work with each other and support each other, and we managed to do that.

We just had to pull together.

We were both like-minded people in the respect that we wanted to see this club succeed and do well, and you didn't want to see it relegated on our watch. But it was a long season, having to look after the team from October, after Ray left, to the end of the season. It was a long time, and not always easy.

There were some huge personalities in that dressing-room and when a group of players have had the success they'd had with Kenny, Ray and Tony, and then two major parts of that group leave, they're looking around and thinking *What's happening here?* And that was the difficult part for us, just stabilising it and keeping it on an even keel until the appointment of Roy Hodgson the following season.

There were some really good days, but there were some dark days as well. You always have dark days in football at times. But Tony was a good man to work with, and we had each other. We knew the way each other worked and it was a relationship that had been built up not over 18 months, but the previous 18-to-20 years.

It was a difficult time, but we managed to do it and the club made strides forward again.

◄◄◄ • ▶▶▶

TONY HAD SPENT nine months steering the ship, before Roy Hodgson swapped Inter Milan for Ewood. And there ensued another overhaul of the squad, but on an even bigger scale than what had been witnessed under Kenny Dalglish.

There was a more continental feel to Blackburn Rovers than Yorkshireman Tony had ever experienced in his time with the club, or indeed in football. But, as always, he took it all in his stride and adapted to the changes that were being implemented and the new faces coming in. He welcomed them all, and was happy to work with them.

Graeme Le Saux, Henning Berg, Paul Warhurst and Nicky Marker were among those who left. They were replaced by Swiss central defender Stephane Henchoz, French right back Patrick Valery, Swedish duo Anders Andersson and Martin Dahlin, and Australian goalkeeper John Filan. And Hodgson appointed an Italian fitness coach, Arnaldo Longaretti, to fine tune them all as they headed back into Europe, albeit securing a UEFA Cup place on the final day of the season.

The additional backroom staff, and Hodgson's own hands-on approach to training at the time, meant Tony's coaching responsibilities were not as intense as they had been the previous season. Hodgson had a different way of working.

But Tony, nevertheless was important to the former Malmo and Switzerland manager.

◄◄◄ • ►►►

Roy Hodgson
(Blackburn Rovers, July 1997-November 1998)

I WAS VERY lucky when I came to Blackburn Rovers from Inter to find a staff of the quality of Tony Parkes, who had done an exceptional job the year before in taking over from Ray Harford and keeping the team in the league, which didn't look at one stage like it was going to happen. But he and Derek Fazackerley did extremely well to keep the team in the league, and I inherited these two people.

Fortunately for me, both were very good characters as well

as very good coaches and, even more importantly perhaps, they knew the club well, they had a good idea of the players and a good understanding of what the players could and couldn't do, which is very helpful when you come into a new club from the outside, albeit that we did have a pre-season so that helped me to come up to speed quicker than maybe if I'd been drafted in during the course of a season.

But Tony was very, very well regarded by everyone at the club, not least of all Jack Walker, with whom he had a special relationship.

And there was no doubt that both he and Derek, but perhaps more so Tony, was a person who was regarded as a Mr Blackburn Rovers-type, having given the club such service both as a player and as a coach.

He was the assistant-manager, of course, and one of two first team coaches.

I didn't share the work out perhaps as much as I should have done in those days, so his role and responsibility would have been making certain that the first team was prepared in the best possible way for the game ahead, but he probably didn't do as much coaching – or Derek for that matter – as they would have liked to do, simply because I stole that part of the work for myself and did so much of it myself.

But, of course, they played an important part in all the decisions we had and discussions we had regarding the team, regarding the players.

I think people who work with you, they do a very important unseen job in the sense that they know what's going on in the dressing-room, the players speak to them perhaps before they come to knock on your door as manager to tell you what they're thinking, so you get a good vibe, if you like, from people like Tony and Derek, who are keeping you informed of the mood in the dressing-room… the way people are reacting to the work that you're doing, and not least of all in terms of team selection. Putting your head together with people like Tony and Derek was very useful for me because they knew the players very well and they could sometimes give me some advice about the players, and help me get to know the players quicker than would have happened than if I'd have just been relying upon the time I was spending with them on the training field.

When I first came into the dressing-room, it wasn't great I suppose, in the sense they'd had such a bad season the season before and been involved in a relegation battle, and had the stress, if you like, of trying to come through that relegation battle, followed by the joy and the euphoria of, 'We haven't lost our Premier League status, we're still here'.

But there were still a lot of very good players that Jack Walker had assembled at the club. We had rather too many centre-halves – we had some really good centre-halves that we had to let go – Chris Coleman was one, Ian Pearce was another, Paul Warhurst was another one, and then we lost Henning Berg to Manchester United.

To lose players of that quality and yet still have the talent we had at the club was quite enormous.

Colin Hendry was obviously a big figure at the club, and we signed Stephane Henchoz and they teamed well together.

I suppose, the other really big characters were the midfield players, and Tim Sherwood, Chris Sutton and Kevin Gallacher as the forwards and, of course, we had Jason Wilcox, who was an important figure, and Stuart Ripley as a wide player. And a very talented young player, Damien Duff, knocking on the door, so it was a quality team, really. We had good players.

We had a good goalkeeper in Tim Flowers.

We had a very good group of players to work with, so it was a strong dressing-room and a lot of those players were quite experienced with a lot of Premier League games behind them.

You couldn't say it was a soft dressing-room.

It was a dressing-room with people with opinions and people who were fully confident about their own ability, and their ability to play in the Premier League. But, luckily, I found them to be a very good group and I would like to think that the relationship between us three – myself, Tony and Derek – and the dressing-room was a good relationship.

I suppose that was proven by the fact that we got into UEFA that year.

◄◄◄ ● ▶▶▶

AFTER HODGSON, CAME Kidd, with Tony again holding the fort for the two weeks or so in between.

◄◄◄ ● ▶▶▶

Kevin Gallacher
(Blackburn Rovers, 1993-99)

WHEN TONY TOOK charge in a caretaker status he relied on us as players to be with him, which we were, but it all boils down to mutual trust. He put a trust in us and we trusted him, and when that happens then it works for you and that's what happened on the pitch.

We came into a football club that was old fashioned... wooden stand, and when the redevelopment was taking place we were getting changed in a building (Blackburn Rovers Indoor Centre – BRIC) next to the ground and getting bussed in on match days. And there was nowhere specific to train.

Tony would be ringing around for football pitches in and around the Blackburn area to try to get a training session on. We didn't have a start time, we didn't have a finish time. And we could be training anywhere... Wilson Playing Fields in Accrington, Pleckgate High School fields, Pleasington fields, British Aerospace, QEGS (Queen Elizabeth's Grammar School)... we even used Accrington Stanley's pitch.

We were sold a dream. When we came to the club, we came for a dream that Jack Walker and Kenny Dalglish had and we hoped that it would be achieved, and that's what happened. What made that dream was Kenny completing the jigsaw, picking people to work with, people that he trusted, people that we trusted and you end up working for each other. And that's how it all happened.

We were all working for each other.

And it was a family club, and Tony was a valued member of it along with Kenny and Ray. Asa Hartford was in there, Alan Irvine, Jim Furnell and Terry Darracott. Tony worked with them all.

I'll always be grateful to him too, for choosing me as captain when he took caretaker charge before Brian Kidd came in.

◄◄◄ ● ►►►

LESS THAN ONE year – and one relegation later – it was all change again.

Hard at work and total concentration in the Rovers dugout

Sir Kenny Dalglish

Alan Shearer

Roy Hodgson

CHAPTER 8

Back to the Premier League... and Worthy Worthington Cup winners

NOTHING COULD EVER eclipse being crowned champions of England. But every achievement, every piece of silverware, meant something to Tony Parkes, because Tony knew exactly what it would mean to the fans and the town as a whole.

Winning promotion back to the Premier League in 2001, working alongside Graeme Souness as his assistant, was special. Securing runners-up spot to Fulham, courtesy of a 1-0 win over Preston in a Lancashire derby at Deepdale, was poignant too coming nine months after the death of Tony's great friend, and the club's benefactor, Jack Walker.

Going on to defy the odds and beat Spurs to lift the Worthington Cup the following season was a remarkable feat. And it was an occasion when, again, Tony's diligence and dedication to Blackburn Rovers was recognised when he was asked to lead out the team at the Millennium Stadium by Souness who – like Dalglish – had seen the immeasurable value and importance of having Tony on the management team.

Souness had vowed to bring the good times back to Ewood Park upon his appointment. And with the help of Tony as his right hand man, he did just that.

◄◄◄ ● ►►►

Graeme Souness
(Blackburn Rovers, March 2000-September 2004)

HE WAS MR Blackburn.

I always think it's imperative that when you take a manager's job, you always have someone there that you can lean heavily on, especially in the beginning to tell you about what you've got in the dressing-room, and Tony was Mr Blackburn.

He knew the club inside out. Also, he can inform you about what sort of group of directors you've got and, just basically, the way the football club is run and any issues you might have going forward.

Tony had great experience, I wasn't the first new manager he'd had to deal with, so he was vastly experienced in what information me or any of my predecessors would have wanted.

He was one hundred percent reliable.

He told you it, as it was, he didn't butter anything up, he was straightforward... he would tell you things you didn't want to hear, and I respected him for that.

He knew the club warts and all, and he would tell you if

he felt we could do things better, and I admired that. Because, sometimes when you're a manager, people just tell you what you want to hear, but he was certainly not that individual.

He would seldom get angry, but he occasionally did with different things, if he thought, 'That's not up to standard, that's not how it should be done'... and he would voice that opinion. There's nothing specific that springs to mind but it would go from team selections to substitutions, to giving the players a day off when he felt they shouldn't be given a day off... or maybe he wanted to give them a day off, when I wanted them to come in.

It was very much a joint effort. Tony was very much part of the decision-making and the day-to-day running of the football club when I was there.

And, of course, it's important to have someone who understands the supporters at a particular football club because they're your paying customer and you try to keep them happy, but of course that sometimes isn't always the case.

It's imperative you have someone who understands, on every level, how that football club is run and where he thinks it can improve. He'd point it out, I might disagree with him on it or I might say, 'Yes, you're one hundred percent correct, we can change that and do that better'.

I leant on him very heavily.

And the fact that I lived in Manchester, and he was on the ground, living in Blackburn, he knew everything that was going on in and around the club and in the town, and he kept me informed all the time.

I can never remember Tony falling out with anyone on the

touchline. He was a class act. He knew his football, he wasn't a confrontational type, but certainly if he felt he had to say something he would *say* something.

He would have been the sounding board for the players. And it wasn't always just football reasons.

When I was a player at Liverpool, we had Ronnie Moran and Joe Fagan. You wouldn't go to Joe with any personal issues, you'd just talk about football. Ronnie Moran was the guy you went to if you needed to talk about anything else, and Tony was that same guy at Blackburn as Ronnie was at Liverpool.

We hit it off instantly. No issues.

John Williams didn't say to me, 'Oh, by the way, you have to keep Tony Parkes'. It was entirely up to me. I relied on him heavily and as far as I was concerned we had a very, very solid working relationship.

We didn't go out socially together, but I enjoyed his company. His humour was dry, typical football humour but dry, and he liked to chuckle. He liked to laugh, and we used to laugh quite a lot, especially when it was going well.

It went particularly well in our first season, winning promotion back to the Premier League at Preston, and it was not long after Jack had died. Sadly, he didn't live long enough to see us get back in the Premier League.

It made for an emotional night, but a great night. We knew what we had to do and we went there and did it. A solid team performance.

We had a really good season that season.

We didn't start too well and John Williams said, 'We can't be playing too much football', but I said, 'Football always wins the day'… and that's exactly what happened. We had a really good season in the end and the players deserve a great deal of credit for getting us up that year.

And Tony backed me up on those discussions with John. He was a football man. He wasn't buying into all the modern techniques and modern terminology. He was a very much from the same school that I went to… a simple game, but people are there trying to complicate it for no good reason other than to make themselves feel better about using certain terminology, hoping to appear more intelligent than they actually are, perhaps.

Tony was very much old school and that's why we hit it off so much.

We were all delighted to get back up.

The Premier League is the place to be. We had good players and I like to think the players came in every day enjoying their work and a lot of that was down to Tony as well because he mixed it up.

And he wouldn't always ask me what we should be doing on a particular day, because I trusted him implicitly.

He took the coaching.

He was the first one in the training ground when I got there. If there were any issues that had developed, he'd be the one to break it to me, non-footballing stuff as well. When you're dealing with 30 young men there are things that crop up occasionally, so he'd be cast with delivering the bad news to me. And he would just shrug his shoulders.

He knew the players better than I did when I first walked

through the doors and there would be things that we'd discuss about the team, talk about things the team or a player had done at a particular ground the previous season, and remind them that they shouldn't be going down that road again… or remind them that they had a really good day there last season, or two seasons ago. They were the little nuggets that only someone who had been involved could come up with.

And when it came to signings, it's a committee thing, so he would have a say in that too. If we needed to strengthen a particular area you'd throw a few names into the hat and you'd take it from there. And, of course, I would ask if he knew him or had any experience of the player and he would either relate a story or say nothing, but he was always asked.

He was a delight to work with.

When you're a manager, you're two people.

When it's going well, you're an open book and everyone's your friend, and when it's not going well you're sort of suspicious and you don't speak to too many people, only the ones very close to you.

But looking back, Tony was consistent.

He treated defeat and success in equal amounts. He never went overboard in either direction, whether we won or lost.

I couldn't be like that.

I was too up and down, and that's ultimately why I chucked it. It wasn't for me. The good times didn't compensate for the bad times.

But the way Tony's mind worked was quite different. He was level-headed and he was really solid. He could take the defeats and success both with a pinch of salt, if necessary. That's why he lasted so long in the game, in that role.

I only have good things to say about him because he was great for me and my four years at Blackburn. We had a really strong working relationship. But it wasn't the sort of relationship where he would have tried to persuade me to stay.

I'm very much someone who, if I make my mind up to do something, I'll stick with it.

But I don't remember that conversation ever taking place.

With the number of managers he worked with, he would have been used to it, and of course he was caretaker manager several times.

I don't know if he ever regretted not being manager himself. He must have thought he could do the job because of the amount of people he was assistant to. I don't know why he didn't push himself forward, when any of us left, to be given a real go at it.

He had the capabilities.

When you're a manager and you get a job within the first five working days, Monday to Friday, by Friday the players fancy you or don't fancy you. They know if you know anything about the game.

Tony sails through that test.

Maybe it was the non-footballing aspects, the politics of football and having to deal with that on a regular basis. I think those two things would have been unattractive to him. But on the training ground and working with players, he loved that. That was his forte.

The way he delivered his message.

He wasn't a shouter, and even when things weren't going well and we'd lost a game, he was consistent and the players liked that. You don't want someone who's up and down and all over the place because of one result. He was consistent.

He did the media duties on occasion for me. He knew all the journalists, they all knew him, and he was cute enough to avoid certain questions. He'd been round the block several times, so he knew the job.

Blackburn was a job that I regretted leaving when I did, I should have stayed a bit longer.

My time at the club was so enjoyable. I worked for good people, I had good people around me, a good group of players, and I think part of the success was Tony's input.

He was a really solid, football man and loved football. And he loved Blackburn Rovers.

That's why I asked him to lead the team out at the Millennium Stadium for the Worthington Cup final.

It was an unbelievable day. No one fancied us.

We didn't have an easy road to the final… with Manchester City, Arsenal and Sheffield Wednesday to play along the way, and then Spurs in the final. And everyone fancied Tottenham. But we always fancied ourselves.

We had some good players in the team.

You've got no chance of being successful unless you've got good senior pros, and I had good senior pros at the club… Craig Short, Brad Friedel, Flitty (Garry Flitcroft) the captain… they were rascals, but they were really solid.

Any issues in the dressing-room, I only got to hear the really important stuff, because the senior players would sort it out before it became an issue, and I would never hear about it. But I was lucky, I had those types with me.

On the day of the final, Brad Friedel made a couple of really good saves. Mark Hughes… we played him in midfield that day, and he ran the show. Andy Cole gets a goal. It wasn't the easiest finish for him. For anyone. I think we deserved to win it.

It was just a great day out. A great stadium to win a competition, great atmosphere in there.

I've won bigger things than the League Cup, but I took tremendous pride in winning that cup because we weren't expected to win it.

We were the small guy going to the final, and the players did themselves proud and their families proud and the club proud to win that trophy. It was a big deal.

We went back to the hotel and had a nice dinner. It was a great night.

Tony went back with the team and I went back to my family home in Hampshire.

Winning the league is the acid test of any football club. Winning the Premier League, I would imagine, that would have been the highlight for Tony. But one special day in a big, special stadium takes some beating as well.

Winning the Premier League with Kenny, though, I think that would be the number one thing he would look back on.

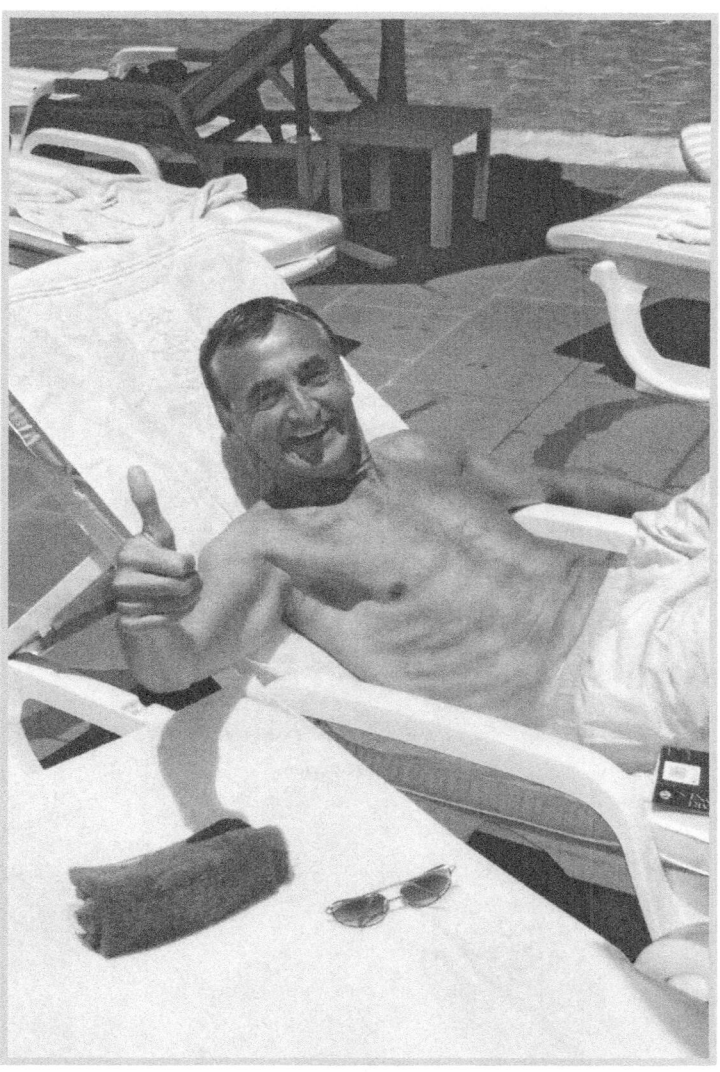

Loving life on holiday in Italy

Graeme Souness

CHAPTER 9

Ewood Exit

NATALIE PARKES DOES not resent football. Not as such, anyway.

When she considers the fact it provided her dad with the only career he had ever wanted, brought achievements and accolades and years of joy, how could she?

But when she reflects on all those years' service, while it gave Tony and his family so much, it deprived them of quite a lot too.

Weekends, especially Saturdays, were work-days for Tony more often than not; school summer holidays did not tally with the football calendar. It was quality, not quantity, when it came to family time.

◄◄◄ • ►►►

NATALIE PARKES

WHEN I MET my husband, Paul, I'd never been to the Lake

District, I'd never been down south, because we used to get just two weeks every year when my dad was off at the same time and we'd go abroad.

We'd go to Spain, Portugal or somewhere. We went to the World Cup in America and in Paris because my dad was doing some work out there, but everything just revolved around football.

There were no weekend or day trips.

So all the things that I do now with Elsie and Matilda, going to Bolton Abbey for the day or to the coast for the day, I'd never done before. I feel like I'm living my childhood through them, because I missed out on an awful lot.

And I don't regret that, I don't kind of look at my dad and think, 'If things would have been different, we'd have done all these things'. I just know there were things that I never did.

We'd never been camping, and it wasn't a case of that they didn't want to, it was never an option.

And things only ramped up once he hit the coaching route, because there's a lot more going on behind the scenes. As a player you just turn up to training and do the training, you turn up to the match and play the match, whereas when you're a coach, you're on the phone a lot more. There's a lot more planning and organising.

I always remember him being on the phone at home talking to other people about problems and different players… and this, that and the other.

My mum couldn't drive, she never learned to drive, so we didn't get to go anywhere. I couldn't do the dance classes when I was little like my friends because it was on the other side of Blackburn, and we couldn't get there because it's not on a bus route, and my dad, of course, was at work.

I think the outsider sees it as this glamorous job and always has, but actually, then – not so much now because of the money that's involved with clubs – but back then it was a sacrifice. My mum was on her own a lot of the time with me... and I think that's why there's only me. Plus the fact I was a difficult baby, by all accounts.

There is honestly no resentment about that.

The resentment I do feel is how Rovers got rid of my dad, because I was the one that told him... I'll never forget it.

I had Radio Lancashire on in the background while I was getting ready for work. I was drying my hair, probably stressing because it wasn't going right, and I turned my hairdryer off just at the point that it came on the news bulletin.

And that's what I heard.

I thought, 'Has my Dad just not told me?'

I wondered if I had heard it right.

I always left for work before he got up, so I had to wake him up to tell him to ring someone because otherwise he would have got ready and gone into work as normal.

That's my resentment. Even now when I've bumped into some of these people who have been extra nice to my dad, I can't look them in the eye, because I think if you think that highly of him why – at that point – couldn't you have just told him?

Yes, he would have been upset, but I think he saw it coming because at one point you're going to have to move on.

But for a reporter to get the news of it first...

We hadn't got a clue.

I had to set off for work, leaving him with that bombshell.

I think after 30-odd years he deserved better than that.

It was never about Mark Hughes, because it's the nature of the game. When they get a new manager they might want to bring in their own backroom staff, that was never the issue, or the fact that he didn't want my dad because he'd got his own people.

It's the fact that there were people at that club who he'd worked with for decades who didn't have the courtesy to just pull him into the office and tell him.

But, typical dad, he took it like he always took things, just in his stride. He's never said a bad word against them. Me and my mum said all the bad words for him. But he respected the decision and he was all right with it.

He wanted to stay in football but I think he was quite glad at having a bit of time off.

My mum and dad went on holiday. They'd always gone to Italy, but this time they went to Majorca and America, and my mum loved having him at home.

But he wasn't ready to retire.

There was a bit of unfinished business.

◄◄◄ • ►►►

TONY PARKES ALWAYS knew, one way or another, the day would come when he would have to leave Blackburn Rovers. But even so, it was too soon when it did.

He had not been ready to walk away from Ewood Park. He certainly was not ready to walk away from football. So when an opportunity arose to reunite with former Blackburn Rovers defender, Simon Grayson, who had made the move into management at Blackpool after ending his playing career with the Tangerines, he took it.

And he was a guiding light to Grayson, who in November 2005 was named as Colin Hendry's successor at Bloomfield Road, initially as caretaker before doing enough to ensure the arrangement was made more permanent.

And in making that transition from player to manager, there was only one man he wanted by his side.

◄◄◄ ● ►►►

Simon Grayson
(Blackburn Rovers, 1999-2002
(Blackpool Manager, 2005-08, 2019-20)

WHEN I GOT the job at Blackpool as caretaker, I knew Tony was out of work, and he was my first port of call when I was told I could get someone in.

I was only 35, and although I had played the game for 20 years, it was my first venture into coaching and managing. I needed someone alongside me who was knowledgeable and understood me; someone I could rely on and trust. That was Tony.

Without Tony Parkes being alongside me in my early years, I don't think I would have made it through over 700 games, with four promotions.

I owe a lot to Tony.

Lads who worked with him, who have gone on to be managers... Tony has had an effect on them with the work that they did with him as players, and the relationship he built with them. They will have taken that on in their own careers. I know I have.

And having him alongside me in those early years at Blackpool was vital.

He wasn't a yes man or someone to agree with me, and he hadn't been that man for Kenny Dalglish or Graeme Souness or any other manager. He was so passionate about the football club and very knowledgeable because he had been in the game so long.

When I first came to Blackburn as a player in 1999, Tony had been around the club for a long time prior to that. I'd actually played against Blackburn Rovers on what would have been a proud day for Tony. I was in the Leicester team in the 1992 play-off final. But it wasn't until 1999 that I got to work with Tony.

He was someone who loved the game, the passion of it all, someone approachable for advice on good things and bad.

But what Tony did best is, he would tell it as it is. If you were having a poor game, he would tell you that, but he would do it in a nice, non-aggressive or hurtful way. It was always done with his mild mannered approach.

I can remember on one occasion at Blackpool there was a presentation night… Gary Taylor-Fletcher was getting an award. He went to Tony and said, 'Why does the manager keep taking me off with 15-20 minutes to go?'

Tony replied, dryly, 'He doesn't take off good players who are playing well'.

Gary didn't know what to say, he just put his head down and walked away. But that was just Tony's dry sense of humour.

If you weren't playing, Tony was someone you could go to and ask why you weren't in the team? It wasn't his decision, of course; when I was there that was down to Graeme Souness or Brian Kidd.

When you aren't in charge, you are the link between the players and the manager, and he would take some of the pressure away from the manager by dealing with all that; dealing with any issues we might have had professionally or personally.

I think that's why so many managers who came in kept him on, because they trusted him. And people above the manager really trusted Tony too. They really valued his opinion and his work ethic.

He was really good in terms of his understanding of the game. He liked people to work hard and have discipline on the training pitch. Because his career got cut short he wanted people to make sure they gave everything, every day, and not let time pass them by, and appreciate everything they have got.

Tactically and technically, he had a good understanding of the game and the different roles within it.

The turnaround that we had at Blackpool… we took on a team that was near the bottom of League One and we survived. We stayed up and we were promoted the following year at Wembley, which was a fantastic experience for everyone. And a big part of those successes was Tony.

We stayed up the following year and then I went to Leeds, but I wasn't allowed to take staff with me.

Tony stepped up, of course. He was so good at that caretaker role.

I never saw him as a number one, he was probably a bit too nice to be a number one. I'm sure if he'd had a go at it he would have given it his best shot. But he was perfect in that role as a buffer, and link between the manager and the players. That was his niche.

He would be out first thing in the morning, setting up all the pitches whatever the weather. One morning it was bouncing down. I looked up from my desk and out of my office window, and I could see him and Steve Thompson trying to move one goal from one end of the pitch to the other. The goals had moved about 200 yards from where they were supposed to be because of the wind.

Tony never bothered, he just got on with it.

He was Mr Steady. He was there day-in and day-out, and so level-headed, so easy to work with, and he offered me so much advice along the way and guidance with his expertise and experience. And I use him as an example to any young managers or head coaches to take someone with you who has been around the game.

I did that with Tony.

I was chuffed that he was voted as Blackburn's favourite son. That's testimony to what Tony did for Rovers.

He is so well respected and highly regarded at the club, and outside of Blackburn too.

◄◄◄ • ►►►

THE RESPECT HE had earned in the game, and contacts too, in over three decades at Ewood Park were of immediate importance to Blackpool.

◄◄◄ • ►►►

Natalie Parkes

THAT WAS A real challenging job from day one. It was like stepping back in time to the 1970s and 80s for dad.

But I think it showed how well respected he was, because when he went to Blackpool there was nothing. I remember him being on the phone to all these different managers saying, 'Who've you got on loan... who can we have?'

In that first team, out of the 11 players, I think only one of them was signed for Blackpool, the rest of them were loaned players. My dad had pulled in every favour.

They managed to sign a few after that, but there was no money.

Even trying to get training facilities, it was like going back to the beginning at Blackburn, playing on public playing fields. Squires Gate was always flooded, so they'd be on the beach or indoors at a leisure centre.

It wasn't the stress of the matches and the games then, it was the stress of all the rest of it.

Half of the players lived on McDonald's three times a day, so it was trying to bring in some of the nutrition but remembering it wasn't a Premier League club.

But, as much as my dad was always quite chilled and funny

and relaxed, he wouldn't hesitate to call anyone out on the football field, and I think he did that quite a lot with Simon.

Obviously, Simon was trying to find his feet as a manager and Dad was never really a 'Yes Man'. He would be happy to go along with stuff if he agreed with it, but if he didn't he would say so.

Eileen and Tony on holiday in Majorca

Ewood Park: Tony returns to the ground (above) after his Alzheimer's diagnosis, and (below) in his 'happy place' with Natalie during a tour of the stadium with the Leyland Sporting Memories Group

CHAPTER 10

A Magnificent Mentor

IT'S FUNNY HOW life sometimes travels full circle.

Especially in football.

Tony had joined a backroom staff at Blackpool that included Steve Thompson, whose dad, Jim was manager of Buxton, and who had actually signed Tony in the 1960s, and was still in charge when he was sold to Blackburn in 1970. Small world.

Tony had always been easy-going, in any company, but there was no question that they would hit it off given the long-standing connection between the two well before they started working together at Bloomfield Road.

Tony had learnt his early trade from Steve's dad, and now it was time to return the favour to another Thompson as he cut his teeth in coaching.

◄◄◄ • ►►►

Steve Thompson
(Blackpool, 2005-14)

HAVING WORKED WITH my dad, Tony went on to become the father-figure for me and Simon as we started our journey in coaching and management.

Tony was assistant to Simon, and I was in charge of the young lads coming through.

We had just finished our playing careers, myself and Simon, so Tony being there was a steadying influence. Everyone wants a good, experienced number two, who you can turn to in different scenarios and different circumstances.

When you're getting into different situations... how to deal with chairmen, how to deal with players, how to sort out contracts, looking at opposition... Tony had been there and done it, we had our ideas as well and we'd bounce things off each other, but sometimes you can't buy that experience that Tony gave us.

Tony had unbelievable experience in football, and at the time that was what myself and Simon needed because it was Simon's first managerial job. I was just coming up through the ranks, coaching the youth team and, obviously, Tony had been there and done it and it was great to have him on board.

Sometimes, you'd think you had to do X, Y and Z, and Tony would say, 'Let's just calm down and think about it rationally' and I think that's what you need, someone with that experience.

You'd watch how he did things and you'd learn from him. You'd learn from his man-management, you'd learn from different sessions that he'd put on, you'd learn how he talked to players...

and that was one of Tony's great strengths.

If you had a problem as a coach and you went to Tony for advice, he'd never belittle you; you could sit down and talk to him, and he wouldn't blind you with science, he'd be calm and collected and really precise.

We were young, me and Simon, and wanted to enjoy our football still and Tony was the calming influence to make sure we made the right decision. He'd let you make the decision, but if he didn't agree, he'd tell you. If he had an opinion, he wasn't scared to tell you… and you'd listen to him.

Equally, Tony was a good listener, and he would be very constructive with how he came back to you.

He had a lovely manner.

He had a side to him that if he wasn't happy he could put you down in one sentence and you knew where you stood with him, without raising his voice.

I remember once we got this lad in on trial based on his unbelievable CV. We got him a kit and got him all set up, but when we went out and looked at him in training, we looked at each other and went, 'Who's brought him in?'

The way he was training didn't reflect his CV at all. I don't think they could have been the same person.

We pulled him into the office at the end to ask how he thought he'd done, and Tony said, 'Can I ask you something? Have you ever played football?'

The lad didn't know what to say, and I had to contain my laughter. But that was Tony. If it needed saying, he could put it over in the right manner.

You knew where you were with him, you knew where you stood. Even the experienced players, and we had some good players at Blackpool like Charlie Adam… even with them, he commanded that respect.

That's the biggest accolade I could give to Tony, people listened to him because of what he'd done in the game.

He had a great sense of humour too. He wasn't one to hold court in front of all the players but he'd chip in with one-liners that were absolutely hilarious.

He's just a likeable football person and there aren't many like Tony Parkes about who are very loyal to one club, like he was with Blackburn. And after that, he was very loyal at Blackpool as well.

Sometimes, loyalty doesn't pay in football, but you could never question his loyalty to Blackburn and what he did.

Tony probably understood at that stage that it was time for him to move on. And with Simon coming to Blackpool, a fresh challenge was probably what he did need to be honest.

And to have Tony on board was Simon's ideal; the experience that he brought, the help he gave us was unbelievable, and he added another promotion to his already outstanding CV when we went up to the Championship. We had good times.

But we had some tough times too, not least when Simon left to go to Leeds.

It didn't faze him, because he'd been there and done it at Blackburn, of course. Whenever the manager moved on or it wasn't going well they had Tony to turn to, for many years. Clubs always need those sorts of people who are there for you, and Tony was always there to steady the ship. That's what he did.

He was a fantastic number two and an experienced coach that people needed around them, and someone who players looked up to. All the members of staff did.

He commanded respect with what he'd done throughout the game. He has an unbelievable CV. When you think about the players he's worked with... at Blackburn especially, some world class players and obviously he won the title with them and all of that.

But even though he wasn't at Blackpool that long really, he's still very fondly thought of there because under tough circumstances and turbulent times, we managed to steady the ship.

We'd lost a lot of players through loans, and Simon left as well. Me and Tony were one and two at Blackpool and we had a great understanding.

We stayed up that year and I thought we'd done enough to deserve a chance to get the job.

◄◄◄ • ►►►

FAMILY CIRCUMSTANCES MEANT that even if the Blackpool job had been offered on a more permanent basis, it is not a role that Tony could have fulfilled.

His world had been turned upside down just before Christmas 2008 when his wife, Eileen, had received a terminal diagnosis of bone cancer. Having kept Blackpool in the Championship, it was time for football to take a back seat.

◄◄◄ • ►►►

Natalie Parkes

IT WAS DECEMBER 22, the day mum was diagnosed.

She'd been having a lot of back and hip pain, which wasn't unusual because she'd had a slipped disc, but she had gone to see the GP about it earlier in the week. They'd tried to get her an MRI scan but there weren't any, so my dad paid to have it done straightaway, and we got a call on the 22nd to say the doctor wanted to see them.

I was cooking tea. They went and they came back both in bits.

I was making pork chops in the pan and I dropped it on the floor. Sauce splattered everywhere on a white kitchen.

I was thinking it might be arthritis, or something along those lines.

I didn't suspect cancer. None of us did. But from day one it was always terminal.

My dad never accepted it.

Ever since they met, they had been inseparable. Outside of football, they did everything together.

They'd met in a nightclub in Sheffield. My mum was actually engaged to somebody else at the time, but she called that off within about a week of meeting my dad, I think. He'd swept her off her feet!

I'm not sure how long she'd been engaged.

I don't know if it's a case of dad making an impression, or if he just made my mum realise that the person she'd been with wasn't right.

Nothing happened until she broke off the engagement, they

just hit it off. But they were like chalk and cheese in a way, from what I remember. Back then, when they used to go out a lot more and they'd go to pubs and restaurants, my mum was probably less anxious.

I think it was probably the move to Blackburn, not knowing anyone, and then when I came along I was a really awkward baby, which doesn't surprise me. So being on your own in an unfamiliar town, with a baby who had problems feeding and all sorts of stuff, I think she felt very alone.

She was probably the wrong person to be a footballer's wife. She didn't like mixing because she never kind of felt good enough. Every Christmas party or anything it was a big deal because she didn't want to be judged by her appearance and she found it really stressful. Once she was there she was fine, but the build-up, the anxiety, the stress, the worry... whereas my dad would just put on a suit and go, like most men do.

I think in the early days, it wasn't so bad because there was no money in the job. But I think once Jack Walker got involved and my mum and dad started mixing with the directors, I think she just always kind of never quite felt good enough – through no one's fault, it was just how she felt.

She wasn't a 'label person' in a fashion sense, but those people were, and I think she felt that they'd know if she wasn't wearing labels.

She'd given up her job at Dolcis to have me, and then when I started school she started work as a dinner lady, which she loved, but she was conscious that it wasn't what she'd imagined as a career and, rightly or wrongly, perhaps she felt judged by that.

None of that ever went on my dad's radar. He didn't over-think things like my mum did, although she didn't always show it.

I think she kept a lot of it to herself until she got diagnosed with cancer, and then she hit him with everything.

I remember one journey back home from hospital, it must have been early on in the diagnosis and they'd given her morphine, which didn't agree with her. It's the only time she'd had morphine, and the night before she'd seen cats on the ceiling and I'd said, 'You need to get her off this medication'.

We were bringing her down off this morphine, and my dad came and she just started having a go at him, about stuff I had no idea about. It was obviously stuff from the past that had built up.

I think a lot of it was about the stuff that they never got to do because he was always at work, and I don't think they'd ever really been in a position to talk about it.

It made my dad cry.

Football was always the thing dad could hide behind. When things got tough, he could just go to work, which you can do with a lot of jobs. He could just go to work rather than face what was happening, and I think that's what he did a lot of when my mum was ill.

But that conversation, I think, that was probably the thing that eventually got him to finish.

*Special Memories: A bitterweet wedding blessing
(above) at the East Lancashire Hospice*

After seven months apart due to the Covid outbreak,
Tony and Natalie finally embrace

CHAPTER 11

One True Love

TONY LOVED, LIVED and breathed football, but the one true love of his life was Eileen.

She died at their home in Wilpshire on October 1, 2009.

He was lost without her.

◄◄◄ • ►►►

Natalie Parkes

I THINK LOSING my mum was the trigger that set off the Alzheimer's for my dad.

I'm not saying it wouldn't have hit us eventually, but it was then he kind of went into himself.

He was always happy in his own company. He didn't always want to be going out, but it was a noticeable change that he didn't want to be around anybody, and I think your brain stops working then when you're not with people.

And with all the dressing-rooms over the years, dad had always been around people. Different types of people from all walks of life.

I would have loved to have been a fly on the wall.

You look at the big characters, like Alan Shearer, Mike Newell, Kenny... I still don't get how my dad could stand his own with those, because they were always playing practical jokes on one another. He loved the banter, and they were always like one big happy family.

I've never heard him call out Mark Hughes. 'You're allowed to, because he was the manager at the time that you left,' I'd tell him.

He never had it in him, which is a nice trait to have.

But with Alzheimer's you get it all taken away, and I'll never really know what he thinks about certain things, because he's not in a position to tell me now.

He never spoke about my mum after she died, because it's not what he does. He bottled up a lot, and he probably did a lot of that to protect me as well.

But then you think *I wonder if he ever did have anyone to talk to?*

Mum's funeral was at Pleasington. I always remember at the church, being quite overwhelmed with the amount of people. Kenny came, there were a lot of people turned up for my dad.

◄◄◄ • ►►►

COLIN HENDRY HAD lost his wife, Denise, earlier that year and reached out.

◄◄◄ ● ►►►

Colin Hendry

TONY SAID TO me, 'You know what it's like'.

But I would never refer to someone losing someone in the same way as it was for me, because every situation is different. You can't compare.

Tony had done so much for us as players we wanted to do what we could to help him.

And that is very much the case now.

◄◄◄ ● ►►►

TONY HAD TIME with his doting daughter, treasured son-in-law, Paul, and later two beautiful granddaughters, but in recent years it has not been in the way that any of them would ever have imagined.

◄◄◄ ● ►►►

Natalie Parkes

THIS SHOULD HAVE been our time.

Making up for time that was lost to football. Weekends away, holidays, days out.

We go to garden centres, now, then we can have a little walk around and there's usually a cafe. My dad loves his coffee so we often go to Costa, or Loom Loft in Clitheroe.

Everything he used to like and do, apart from football, he's not interested in anymore.

Keep fit type stuff, cricket… he loved golf, he can't stand it now.

He did a lot of running. He didn't mind reading and doing crosswords, and now he won't.

He can't focus.

He can read the individual words but can't put them together to get the meaning, and I think that's the same watching TV.

He likes music… Rod Stewart, my mum's favourite… Neil Diamond, Elton John. Lively music.

He seems to remember lyrics and tunes.

He enjoys going to the Sporting Memories groups and one of the volunteers, Janet, takes him to football matches and some events. But it hurts because he's the opposite of how I always remember him. I never remember him being sad or anxious, he was always just fun.

He was never a joker at home and he wouldn't ever play practical jokes, but he was quick and he'd just come out with stuff. It was often just his comebacks, but he'd say it without any expression.

He'd never be caught out with anything, he'd always have a response, and every now and again you do get a glimmer of that still.

I remember being blown away by his wedding speech because it was hilarious, and I didn't actually realise he was that funny.

How he'd written it... because he finished school quite early his English and his grammar were never that good, and he'd always write in capital letters.

I got married when my mum was ill and he tested his speech out on the hospice staff. And I still can't believe he'd actually written it. I'd never heard him speak about anything other than football!

It was observations about me and Paul. I met Paul on holiday the summer I was going to university straight after A-levels. Paul's five years older than me, and my dad just went mental.

I'd never seen him like that.

Paul lived in London, so when Paul came up here he had to stay at our house and my mum insisted that he stayed at the house, so she could keep an eye on us.

I think the first time he came, my dad was away, but the second time my dad was around and it was the only time I've ever seen him not welcoming, and being a really hard nut to crack. He was like a different person because I think he thought that I'd drop out of Uni for Paul.

I didn't, I went to Leeds and I finished my degree, and Paul won him round eventually. Although I think we'd probably been going out for about a year before that happened!

Paul is from North London but his dad was from Liverpool, and Paul is a Liverpool fan, so they always had that talking point.

We once picked him up from a train station one Friday night and Kenny was there too, to pick up one of the girls. So my dad and Kenny were talking, and Kenny was saying, 'I hope he's brought flowers'.

'He won't have brought flowers,' I replied. 'He's come from work', so Paul gets off the train, a Liverpool fan, and Kenny goes straight up to him and starts having a go at him for not having any flowers.

Paul's face was a picture. He didn't have a clue what to say at all. Then, all the way in the car, all he could say was, 'That was Kenny!'

That's how I like to remember my dad, just doing what dad's do.

◄◄◄ • ►►►

NATALIE NOTICED THE changes in Tony.

As a family, they have always been very private, but there came a point when she felt people needed to be aware of her dad's condition because of the change in his personality.

◄◄◄ • ►►►

Natalie Parkes

WHENEVER WE WENT away for summer holidays, no matter where we went, we'd always meet someone who knew who dad was, and you'd be dodging them then for the rest of the holiday.

Dad could talk about football until he was blue in the face, so it didn't ever really bother him, it was my mum who used to get annoyed because they just had that two weeks a year where they got to go on holiday together.

We went somewhere like Tuscany once and we still bumped into someone.

That was part of what made me go public with dad's diagnosis, because people would go up and talk to him, and they might not understand what was wrong. Sometimes, he could be rude or other times he'd just be vacant. I just thought if I let people know, it won't stop them approaching him but it will help them to understand how he is and the reason why. Because his personality became so different.

It was Andy Bayes from Radio Lancashire who suggested speaking about it. I didn't realise how far it would go once I did that interview with him. But it has been fairly helpful to have people know.

When I have approached people, you don't have to go through the whole story because it's already out there. It's a shame that you have to go public, but it has helped because, apart from Paul, I am on my own with it.

I've got children and you have to pull yourself together that bit more, but I dropped to six stone when my mum died. I have a photograph that I always keep on my phone and it's to remind me not to be that person.

I stopped eating, I stopped doing anything, I was just so sad. It was nine months from diagnosis... and I got married in the middle of that.

I feel like every moment since my twenties has just been stolen.

I had Elsie, and then with Matilda because of lockdown and everything with dad, I couldn't enjoy it in the same way as I should have.

It's been endless.

It's taken me a long time to come to terms with what happened with my mum because she was my best friend. We did everything together.

All she ever wanted was to enjoy her retirement, and she never got it, and neither has my dad.

I think with not having any siblings as well, it's difficult. It all falls on you to deal with.

Paul lost his mum very quickly after I lost mine.

Cancer was cruel. Alzheimer's feels like losing dad twice, because you know that day is coming… but part of him has gone already.

Elsie Mae's Christening at St Peter's Church, October, 2018
(above), and Tony actually meeting his first grandchild

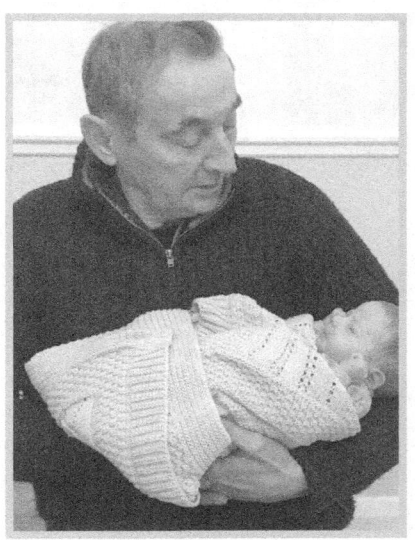

Lockdown Life... Brungerley Park, Clitheroe, May, 2020

CHAPTER 12

Home from Home

THERE WERE MIXED emotions when Natalie discovered she was pregnant with her second child in early 2020.

For medical reasons, her first born, Elsie Mae, had been a miracle. Natalie had not imagined being blessed again.

Throw in the added complications of coronavirus and lockdown, and she was left with the toughest of choices – keep her dad at home, where there were potential risks, or arrange some respite.

It felt like a lose-lose situation for her.

◄◄◄ • ►►►

Natalie Parkes

IT WAS ALL a bit of a whirlwind.

To have Matilda, I looked into respite for my dad, and it was never ever meant to be a permanent thing. I never thought of it as like *Oh let's look at respite and then maybe he'll stay.* It literally was meant to be three months, and then he was coming home.

And I was so devastated when I dropped him off, but in my mind then he was definitely coming home.

I must have cried for two days solid.

The house was so quiet and it felt wrong because it was in the middle of Covid, and so it was a drop-off and then I couldn't see him, especially when I was going in to hospital myself to have Matilda. It wasn't as if I was allowed to see him.

But as soon as I brought Matilda home it became really clear that I couldn't do it all.

There was no way.

We'd had months of dad breaking down doors and trying to get out of locked windows, and how can you deal with that when you're feeding a baby?

I think at first I'd forgotten how hard it is to have a new baby and how often they feed, and I thought *Oh, it will be fine...* because I knew they slept a lot.

But then I thought *What would I do in the middle of a feed and my dad's trying to get out of the window?*

What happens if I'm busy with Matilda and he leaves the front door open?

And Elsie, who was two and a half at the time, gets out?

I just spent nights thinking... *What if, what if, what if?*

And it could have just been a *What if.*

But the risk was too high.

I actually spoke to the health visitor one time I saw her, and she said that basically if my dad stayed, we'd have more input from social services from a safety point of view.

So that kind of gave me food for thought as well because I couldn't have that pressure, and that kind of chaos in our lives.

Initially, I just extended it. The respite.

We were in the middle of a pandemic, there was nowhere else for him to stay.

I had no choice but to keep him there. And then, as time went on, he did settle and he was all right. And I think once I saw him there, I had no other choice but to leave him there.

But the guilt is just…

I feel guilty because I told my mum I'd look after him.

He is happy there, and he's fine.

He likes being around people, more so now than he ever did, and there are always people there.

Whereas here, I'm always busy.

You're always trying to juggle something.

The girls kind of understand a bit more when you're busy making tea or doing housework, whereas my dad just wanted to go out all the time.

Finding the home was definitely the right decision. It's just hard because he changes so much… so quickly.

It just adds to the guilt, because I felt like I literally dropped him in a place that he'd never seen before, because Covid stopped us going to have a look around… with people he'd never met… and then I walked away.

We tried a window visit once and he got really upset, so we stuck to FaceTime, but all he kept saying was, 'Where have you been?' Seeing him for the first time after seven months, in PPE and masks... I wasn't sure he really recognised me because of all of it... and he had to wear gloves, and he found that hard because he kept wanting to take them off.

But just to be able to physically hold his hands, even though we weren't meant to, is something I'll never forget.

You never know how fast things deteriorate. I kept thinking *He's going to forget me...* and you don't get that back. Once it's gone, it's gone. And for my dad it makes that difference, that social contact.

He's very vacant without it.

The first time I saw him, the change in him was immense, and then you feel guilty all over again because you think if he'd have stayed with us, would it be this bad? But the home is bigger, with more people.

The next battle after seeing him was that he wanted to go out, but it was months and months before they were allowed to go out and he didn't understand.

The first indoor activity that we did after Covid, we went to a painting cafe with the girls and I said to dad, 'You pick one'... and he picked a football, obviously.

He really enjoyed concentrating and painting.

He would have hated doing that before.

His language is very limited now. I think he understands a lot more of what you say to him than what he can give back. And I think that sometimes causes him a lot of frustration, that he doesn't know how to answer things.

I don't think he knows exactly who I am anymore.

He knows I'm something to do with him and he knows I'm important, but if I went without either of the girls he doesn't always recognise me straightaway.

He recognises the girls more than anything. And Elsie's the only name he still knows.

He doesn't remember being married. I show him a photo of my mum and the memory is not in that part of his brain.

The only thing really he's got is football, because when he watches football, something is still there.

He'll cheer at the right places, he'll point at the right places, as if that is so embedded in his brain that it's kind of innate. He wouldn't necessarily have a clue who's playing.

He knows it's Rovers if they're in blue and white, but when he watched one of the 2022 World Cup semi-finals he was cheering in the right places but he'd no idea who was actually playing.

The only place you see him relax is Ewood Park.

You just see it in him.

As soon as you take him down the M65 and come down towards Ewood, as soon as he sees the floodlights, his shoulders go down and he just changes.

I think he's just spent so long there over the years, it feels like home.

◄◄◄ • ►►►

FITTINGLY, TONY GETS a name-check and features in the video of Ewood Lights – a song written by Rovers' fan, Jacob Reddy, the proceeds of which go towards the 'Remember the Rovers' initiative *which supports local residents aged over 50 who are living with dementia or those feeling isolated or vulnerable.*

The group meets weekly and is attended by Tony.

Charity football matches have been arranged to raise funds for his ongoing care, as well as dementia and other charities. Blackburn Rovers have hosted dinners and reunions in recognition of service.

A crowd-funder set up by a Rovers fan so that fans can help care for the caretaker has raised thousands.

His football family have rallied round in his time of need, and Natalie is eternally grateful. She feels let down, however, by those who should have stepped up.

◂◂◂ • ▸▸▸

Natalie Parkes

I FOUND I was just going round in circles with the PFA (Professional Footballers' Association).

Any support from the PFA stopped for dad after Gordon Taylor left but, thankfully, Blackburn Rovers and the Rovers fans stepped in to show their support and gratitude to dad last year. Wherever he goes locally, people clap and cheer.

It makes him smile and in some ways this helps him to remember who he is. He is loved by the people of Blackburn, and because of this his legacy will continue to live on.

It means a lot to me to know how much people love and respect him but, equally, it's hard as I miss this man.

I don't think dad would ever truly understand what he

achieved in his career. He just saw it as a series of being in the right place at the right time and him being lucky, because he actually got to live out his childhood dream.

It was just a job to him.

He never wanted to be manager full-time.

Never once.

They had tried to give it him twice during his successful stints but he just didn't ever want to be the manager.

I don't think he ever wanted to be the one to make the decisions, to be in front of the press, even though he was always really comfortable talking to the press and being on the radio – it never fazed him, and often Kenny would make him do that. He just didn't want that responsibility full-time. He never wanted the glory.

Dad's strengths lay in other areas.

He loved working with the players on the training ground, getting the best out of them.

Dad tried not to have favourites, but if you were to ask him today it would be Alan Shearer.

He'd never seen anyone in real life with so much skill.

To him, he was just the best thing he'd ever seen, and I think because he was such a nice guy to go along with it, that helped as well.

He had a soft spot for Damien Duff too and really helped him when he was younger. Damien was so homesick for his family back in Ireland, he was ready for going home.

Dad put so much effort in to keep him at Blackburn, and the club used to fly Damien's parents over to visit because they knew if he went back home he might never come back. So they had to build up his confidence enough to be in a position where he was happy to stay, and dad played a part in that.

Damien just missed his family because that's all he'd known. Then all of a sudden he just settled.

Dad got a lot of satisfaction from seeing the young players come through.

He got more invested in them.

Dad always had a soft spot for the hard workers, like Colin Hendry, too. He liked Mark Atkins as well. They weren't necessarily the best players but they worked hard.

I think he saw a bit of himself in Mark as well, because when he arrived at Blackburn, he was playing in a different position, as my dad had. But he changed Mark's role in the team.

Dad always had that knack of just being able to see where people should be and where they are better suited.

He saw the potential in people and wanted them to do well. He wanted to make sure that every player that played had a fair crack at it.

There was never anything as a lost cause to him.

Obviously, there would have been some that no matter how hard you try, it just doesn't work out. But I think, with Blackburn being at the time a small family club, you got a lot of players that came and stayed.

It wasn't like it is now – very in and out, they stay a couple of seasons and they go. A lot of players when my dad was there, were there for a long time.

As well as a good coach, dad was a confidante for a lot of them.

He was there a lot for people who had problems, not so much in football but out of it, especially when he was at Blackpool. There were an awful lot who had money problems and this and that.

It's a side of football that you don't necessarily see. But if people want that career enough they need to sort that side of things out. Dad played his part in that.

He was always good at listening.

He wouldn't say much, but he could be in the room, things could be happening around him and it's as if people didn't realise he was there and he was taking it all in.

They knew he wouldn't go and grass them up, but he would deal with things in the right way.

They always trusted him.

I suppose it's only now I'm really reflecting on what dad did and what he achieved.

It's weird because partly it helps with the Alzheimer's, because I know he isn't going to be forgotten, but then it makes me sad because there are a lot of people out there in the same position with Alzheimer's and dementia who will never have that opportunity because the nature of their jobs mean that their memories just fade away.

For us, there are enough people and enough photographs to keep those memories alive

We've got loads of pictures at home but they're in a box in the loft that I've not opened since we lost mum.

It's hard enough looking back at pictures of my mum now she's not here anymore. But now I find looking at pictures of my dad is hard too because it's not the same person.

It's just weird.

I don't know how long this is going to go on for, and how much of a decline we're going to go through before the end point.

Sometimes, you just think 'Why make them suffer?'

I know there's a point where they don't know enough to realise any different, but my dad does know that he can't do things and that he struggles with things, and you just wonder why make him suffer so much.

I do believe his illness is football-linked. But equally, I can't go blaming football like some other people do. Everyone's got their own opinion.

My dad loved that life and hindsight is a wonderful thing. They can't change what's happened, all they can do is try to make sure that the modern game is safer, which I think it is because of the nature of the game… the balls, the pitches, all the fitness that is inherent in the modern game.

There are so many ex-players you hear about getting diagnosed now and it's all from that 60s and 70s era, because they knew no different. There was no medical guidance about it.

My dad won't understand, thankfully, what's happening to him and how everything has changed. He just knows he can't do certain things.

But it hurts because he's the opposite of how I always remember him. I never remember him being sad or anxious, he was always just fun.

He was never emotional, but if I needed a hug he'd always know when to hug me.

You used to be able to make him laugh, but now you can't. The

Alzheimer's, however it manifests, has done that.

Football is the one thing that gives him a spark.

Being at Ewood.

That's his happy place. It always has been.

*Natalie gets some time with her dad (above) after Rovers'
game against Chesterfield had been called off, and (below)
father and daughter relaxing at home in the sun*

'I Love my Grandad' by Elsie Mae (aged 5)

EPILOGUE

Tony in his own Words

IN AN INTERVIEW he gave to the club back in 2005, Tony Parkes reflected on his remarkable 34-year association with Blackburn Rovers, which included spells as a player, coach and caretaker manager, and culminated in the club's Premier League title triumph in 1995...

Tony, take us back to the very beginning and how your move to Rovers from Buxton in 1970 came about?

I remember travelling up from Sheffield, my home town, to Ewood and walking up Nuttall Street to a portakabin in the car park, just opposite the office. My first game was against Manchester United, which I think we won 4-1.

A player called John Connelly, who had been involved in the 1966 World Cup winning squad, was with Rovers at the time and he was playing for the reserves that night and scored a hat-trick!

I played a part in two reserve games, obviously did okay and then signed on. Blackburn was only a small club in those days.

We had no money and were always in the lower leagues – yo-yoing between the Second and Third Divisions. It was only really when Jack Walker and Kenny Dalglish got involved that it became a high-profile club.

Gordon Lee played a key role in your development as a player. Talk to us about him and his time in charge?
Gordon was one of the most popular managers I think we've ever had here at Rovers. He was certainly one of the best managers around at lower level football. Gordon came from Port Vale and assembled a good team together.

He knew the players, he knew what kind of players to buy and, of course, he led us to the Third Division title in that memorable 1974-75 season. Winning the Third Division Championship with Gordon at the helm was excellent. We had some really good games during that season.

We were always in contention with Plymouth at the time and one of the greatest games of that era – people still stop me to talk about it – came against Plymouth at Ewood when the race for the title was really starting to hot up. We beat them 5-2 after being 2-0 down – it didn't guarantee us the Championship, but it certainly gave us a push in the right direction. Great days, but very different days.

There wasn't a lot of money around and so when we played away from home, if we won, the directors or the chairman would stop the coach at a pub and we would all have a drink for half-an-hour or so. That was your treat, that was your bonus. It was probably a happier and certainly a less pressured time.

You were allowed to lose games, it wasn't the end of the world if you got beat. They were not constantly gunning for the manager after he'd lost a game. Out of all the managers I worked for, Gordon is certainly the one that stands out the most. When he left for Newcastle, there were eight players who went round to his house to ask him not to go.

He was always very popular with the players and everyone wanted him to stay, but the lure of top-flight management was too good to turn down.

How did it feel to be appointed captain under Jim Smith?
Being made captain was a great honour. Everyone you talk to wants to be captain of their club. I enjoyed it with Jim, we had a good team in those days and we played some great attacking football, so it was a good time to be captain. Jim was a good man, he called a spade a spade.

He was quite a tough character, he used to bounce a few cups around, but he never held grudges or let arguments run on for longer than a day.

You eventually moved into coaching under Howard Kendall, as player-coach of the reserves at the age of 30. How did you find that?
Coaching the reserves was difficult, as both the reserves and the first team usually played on a Saturday, so somebody else had to take charge on the day of a game.

You then became caretaker manager for the first time in 1986, following Bobby Saxton's departure. How was that?

It was a little bit daunting to be honest. My first game was against Portsmouth at home and we won 1-0. I was in charge for four league games, none of which we lost, before Don Mackay took over. Together, we won the Full Members' Cup in 1987.

People don't recognise it, but for Blackburn that was a big event. We took 27,000 fans to Wembley and it was a fantastic day. We were in and out of the play-offs and with him as manager and me as coach, we did very well. Bobby was more hands on when it came to training, whilst Don left the training more to me. He used to watch and then step in when he had something to say.

You were back at Wembley for the 1992 play-off final and Kenny Dalglish asked you to lead out the team. That must have been a special occasion?

Leading the team out in front of 68,000 fans was a very special and emotional moment for me. Not only did we win, but the league system changed that year and so from Division Two we found ourselves playing Premiership football the following season.

Kenny's arrival at the club and Jack's growing involvement marked a new chapter in Rovers' history. What Kenny achieved in those three-and-a-half years was sensational. After gaining promotion, we signed Alan Shearer for a British transfer record fee of £3.3m and finished fourth in the 1992-93 season. We then came second in the 1993-94 season and qualified for Europe for the first time in the club's history. Then, who can forget the 1994-95 championship-winning season that landed us in the

Champions League. We seemed to attract a lot of bad press during those days.

A lot of people were jealous of the fact that a small town club had won the Premiership and said it was only down to Jack's millions. That was unfair. We won because we had a great manager, a good team spirit and we amassed more points than any other team. It was a shame to see Kenny leave the following season, it would have been interesting to see how far he could have taken this club.

Was Kenny the best manager you ever worked with?

The Kenny Dalglish era saw Blackburn Rovers move onto a new level. Because Kenny was such a big name in football, he attracted high-profile players to the club. Winning the Premiership title was just fantastic. He was a great man to work with and those three years with him were probably the most exciting this club has ever seen.

Who is the best player you have ever coached?

It would have to be Alan Shearer. He was a striker who just loved scoring goals and from the day he arrived at the club everyone knew he was going to be a special player. Some strikers who you work with will shoot wide fairly regularly in training, but with Alan it was very rare if you ever saw him miss the target.

He was a very single-minded, old-fashioned, strike, who wanted wingers to put crosses in for him all day long. He scored over 30 league goals a season for three years running and that kind of record speaks for itself.

Finally, how would you sum up Jack Walker and his contribution to this club?

Jack was a football man and a massive Rovers fan. He said to me one day, 'The only thing I want to see is Blackburn in Europe and to have my own box at Ewood, so I can bring my family and my guests' – he got that wish. He never said that much, but he just wanted what was best for the club.

You don't get that kind of money by being a soft touch and he would spend a lot of money bringing players to the club, but he wanted success. He did wonders for this club and he did wonders for the town of Blackburn. He brought a lot of work and publicity to the area, and I'm sure the people of Blackburn have got a lot to thank Jack for, because I know that I have.

In the space of about three years, Jack built Ewood Park, the training facilities and the Academy at Brockhall and a championship-winning side... something that it takes most clubs a lifetime to achieve.

Made in United States
North Haven, CT
19 July 2023

39271686R00104